FINANCIAL REPORTING TECHNIQUES IN
20 INDUSTRIAL COMPANIES
SINCE 1861

Richard Vangermeersch

University of Florida
Accounting Series Number 9

UNIVERSITY PRESSES OF FLORIDA

Gainesville 1979

University of Florida Accounting Series No. 9
Williard E. Stone, Series Editor

School of Accounting, University of Florida
Robert F. Lanzillotti, Dean
John K. Simmons, Director

The editorial content of this work has been evaluated
by the editorial committee of the School of Accounting,
University of Florida, and the book has been approved
for publication by the Board of Managers, University
of Florida Press.

Published through the Imprint Series, Monograph
Publishing. Produced and distributed by University
Microfilms International, Ann Arbor, Michigan 48106.

University Presses of Florida is the scholarly book
publishing agency of the State University System
of Florida.

Library of Congress Cataloging in Publication Data

Vangermeersch, Richard G   J
 Financial reporting techniques in 20 industrial
companies since 1861.

 (University of Florida accounting series ; no. 9)
(Monograph publishing : Imprint series)
 1. Financial statements—United States—History.
2. Accounting—United States—History. I. Title. II. Series:
Florida. University, Gainesville. School of Accounting.
University of Florida accounting series ; no. 9.

HF5601.F55 no. 9   [HF5681.B2]   657'.08s
ISBN 0-8130-0624-4   [657'.3'0973]   79-1238

TABLE OF CONTENTS

Introduction

The first *Accounting Trends and Techniques* was published in 1948 for the period 1946-47. (1) A researcher can glean much about what has happened in financial accounting in annual reports from 1946 to now by examining *Accounting Trends and Techniques* through the subsequent years. This study gives researchers a reference for financial accounting happenings in annual reports long before the middle 1940's and should help them make more definitive statements about financial accounting and should serve as a synopsis of the history of financial accounting for the United States.

Louis Goldberg inspired this study in his monograph, *An Inquiry into the Nature of Accounting:*

> In the English speaking countries--and in others, of course--there are available numerous published financial reports of enterprises--companies whose shares are dealt in on stock exchanges, public utilities, government departments and instrumentalities. Admittedly, there are many enterprises whose reports are not made available to the public, but those in the categories mentioned above constitute a considerable proportion of the national economy. It must also be recognized that the quality of presentation of the information and the extent of data included in these reports vary according to local and even individual practice, and this must be taken into consider-

ation in comparing results of different units and categories. Nevertheless, there is here a vast reservoir of information which has been tapped only to a slight extent to date—source material for research which can be adequately undertaken only by people with some training in and knowledge of accounting.

There is, in short, a need for many dispassionate and detailed studies of accounting data and of accounting procedures, by investigators trained in research methods; this work requires patience and diligence, and much of it may appear, on a superficial view, trivial and inconsequential. But, apart altogether from the interchange of information between specialists that this would provide, who knows when a Darwin might arise to gather the many threads together and weave them into a cloth of grand pattern and enveloping utility? Better to have a superabundance of material on which he shall be able to use his selective discrimination than to frustrate his efforts by an absence of empirical data. (2)

In order to fulfill Professor Goldberg's wish, the writer reviewed the catalog of the annual report holdings at the Baker Library at Harvard and selected 20 industrial companies for an analysis of their financial accounting events. Railroads and other public utilities were considered outside the scope of this study, because of the tradition in financial accounting of considering them separately from industrials. The companies chosen and the first year in which a report was present at the Baker Library were:

1	The American Bank Note Company	1906
2	American Ship Building Company	1900
3	Armour	1910
4	Calumet & Hecla Mining	1884
5	Diamond International	1899
6	E.I. DuPont de Nemours	1907
7	Eastman Kodak	1902
8	General Electric	1893
9	General Motors	1911
10	Hart, Schaffner & Marx	1911
11	International Business Machines	1911
12	International Harvester	1907
13	(S.S.) Kresge	1912
14	Nabisco	1899
15	Pullman and Company	1875
16	Quincy Mining	1861
17	Union Oil	1903
18	Uniroyal (U.S. Rubber)	1893

| 19 | United Brands (United Fruit) | 1900 |
| 20 | U.S. Steel | 1902 |

The companies were chosen because of length of time they had been reporting, the completeness of their report files at Baker Library, and the goal of covering companies in as many different industries as possible. The writer examined each annual report through the 1969 annual report, except for Calumet & Hecla Company, whose last report in the Library was 1967. There were six major topical areas and one general area. They were:

01	Balance Sheet Presentation and Philosophy
02	Income Statement Presentation and Philosophy
03	Earned Surplus and Extraordinary Items
04	Depreciation
05	Inventory
06	Valuation of Fixed Assets
07	Other Matters

The writer then prepared a chronology of these topics by company with many excerpts taken directly from the annual reports. This chronology is the basis for the analysis which follows the general format of the first *Accounting Trends and Techniques.*   The writer utilized tables to tighten the presentation and made some comments on controversial findings.

TOPIC 1
BALANCE SHEET PRESENTATION
AND PHILOSOPHY

1 Balance Sheet Format

It is evident that some sort of balance sheet disclosure was regarded as a usual reporting practice. Sixteen of 20 companies always presented complete balance sheets in one of the three formats of either fixed assets first, current assets first, or current assets minus current liabilities (see Table 1, p. 70). The four companies which did not always present a balance sheet were Quincy Mining, Calumet & Hecla, Pullman, and Union Oil.

Quincy Mining (#16) from 1861 to 1937, when a reorganization was affected, presented its balance sheet in two separate statements. For example, in 1861, the first statement listed expenditures and receipts since the company's inception and was balanced by a debit balance for cash on hand and a credit balance for notes payable. The second statement listed liabilities of notes payable, drafts unpaid, unpaid charges on copper on hand, and accounts payable at mine, totaling $202,685.52. The assets were listed as cash on hand, copper on hand, cash on hand at mine, accounts receivable at mine, available supplies, and balance (of liabilities over assets), totaling $202,685.52.

Calumet & Hecla Mining (#4) in 1884 had a balance sheet composed of assets (cash at Boston, cash at mine, copper, and bills receivable), of liabilities (drafts in transitu, notes payable, accounts payable, and loans payable), and of excess of assets. In the 1900 annual report no balance sheet was issued. In 1901, balance sheet disclosure resumed. The format continued until 1923, when a re-

1

organization occurred. In 1900, Pullman and Company (#15) condensed its balance sheet to the amounts of net assets, surplus, and
capital stock. This policy continued until 1906. Union Oil (#17) in
1903 listed its resources but the company deemed it unwise to furnish
a complete balance sheet. In 1904, no such listing was made. In
1906, a listing was made of corporations in which Union Oil had a
controlling interest. In 1911, a balance sheet was disclosed.

All the 20 companies had adopted the current asset first format
by 1939. Eight of the companies then switched to the current assets
minus current liabilities format but 4 of these companies later
reverted to the current assets first format.

2 Comparative Balance Sheets

By 1966, the 20 companies all had comparative balance sheets.
An analysis of the dates of the first comparative balance sheets and
of the year in which the policy, once adopted, was dropped indicates
that it was a long time before comparative balance sheets became a
usual reporting practice (see Table 1, p. 70).

3 Position of Prepaid Expenses Account

The placement of the prepaid expenses item by the companies
was a surprise.   Hendriksen wrote that "the reporting of prepaid
expenses is a product of the traditional accounting structure."

> Prepaid expenses were included in the definition
> because if they had not been acquired, they would require
> the use of current assets in the normal operations of the
> business. But, in this regard, they are the same as
> inventories; both would require the use of current funds if
> they had not been acquired previously. The main reason
> for their inclusion is that they represent resources
> committed for only a short period--the current operating
> cycle. Like inventories, they result in current funds
> becoming available for recommitment through the sale of
> the product or services and the collection of the proceeds.
> However, the reporting of prepaid expenses is a product of
> the traditional accounting structure. Little economic
> interpretation can be obtained from this information and
> it is doubtful that it can be helpful to investors in their
> prediction and decision activities. (3)

Six of the 20 companies have always classified prepaid expenses
as an other asset, while Diamond International, General Electric,

General Motors, and Pullman and Company started with the prepaid expenses item as a current asset but then switched to and remained with the other asset classification (see Table 1, p. 70). The remaining 10 companies finally adopted the current asset position in 1947, 1948 (2), 1950, 1957, 1959 (2), 1960 (2), and 1961. This finding casts some doubt on the traditional theory of the placement of prepaid expenses as a current asset. These companies appeared much more influenced by the placement recommended by the Federal Reserve Board in its 1917 "Uniform Accounting" pamphlet, in which prepaid expenses were listed as a deferred charge, a noncurrent asset, (4) than the 1947 recommendation of the American Institute of Accountants in ARB #30 that prepaid expenses be classified as a current asset. (5)

4 First Mention of Current Assets on the Balance Sheet

The first use of the term current assets as a caption in the balance sheet ranged from 1900 to 1937. The distribution was 1900 (1), 1902 (2), 1906 (1), 1907 (1), 1910 (1), 1911 (2), 1912 (2), 1913 (2), 1914 (1), 1915 (1), 1917 (2), 1922 (1), 1925 (1), 1927 (1), and 1937 (1) (see Table 1, p. 70).

5 Use of Parenthetical Notation of the
Market Value of Marketable Securities

Fifteen of the 20 companies included the market value of marketable securities in the balance sheet by a parenthetical notation. One company, Eastman Kodak (#7), did this as early as 1908 and DuPont (#6) adopted it in 1920. Thirteen of these companies adopted this practice between 1919 through 1946. They were: #2 (1929), #13 (1931), #19 (1932), #5 and #20 (1933), #1, #4, #15, and #18 (1934), #14 (1935), #17 (1937), #9 (1939), and #11 (1946).

6 Current Assets Listed in Inverse Order of Liquidity

Twelve of the companies listed current assets in the inverse order of liquidity. These companies were: #1 (1906-34), #2 (1914-15), #3 (1910-21), #5 (1913-36), #7 (1902-28), #8 (1917-32), #10 (1911-24), #12 (1907-27), #13 (1913-33), #15 (1925-29), #17 (1912-16), and #20 (1902-38). It is evident that the inverse order of liquidity listing of current assets was a fairly strong tradition for some of these 12 companies.

7 Accounting for Subsidiaries in Unsettled Times

The problem of how to account for subsidiaries in countries embroiled in World War II brought about various solutions for some of the companies--American Bank Note (#1), Eastman Kodak (#7), International Business Machines (#11), International Harvester (#12), and United Fruit (#19). All these companies had important commitments in fixed assets in foreign countries. This item overlaps somewhat with item #20, income of unconsolidated subsidiaries.

In 1939, American Bank Note portrayed its balance sheet with two columns, company and consolidated, because of the unsettled conditions in Europe. This policy continued until 1953. In 1939, Kodak removed its wholly owned German subsidiary from its consolidation and reported the cost of the investment in a new caption, "investments in wholly owed subsidiary companies not consolidated." This account increased in 1940 to $23.461 million by adding Kodak subsidiaries and branches in England, France, Denmark, Holland, Romania, Italy, Hungary, Switzerland, Belgium, Portugal, Japan, and Yugoslavia. In 1941, the investment in most of the companies was written off to the reserve for contingencies account. In 1947, these investments were brought back into the records. Kodak reclassified its reserve for contingencies in 1949 to a contra-asset account of $12.671 million to the investments in and advances to subsidiary companies and branches not consolidated. In 1967, foreign holdings were again consolidated. By the end of 1966, the company's equity in its subsidiary companies outside the United States was $329.487 million, compared with the balance sheet valuation on a cost basis of $70.026 million.

IBM handled the pre-World War II foreign problems in this manner in 1935. "The company includes in its consolidated earnings the undistributed earnings of its foreign subsidiaries. Due to the difficulty in getting remittances from foreign countries, owing to foreign governmental exchange restrictions, a reserve has been set aside in the amount of $722,000, the full amount of the blocked net profits." By 1942, this reserve had reached the amount whereby a $1.00 valuation was shown for the investment account. In 1940, International Harvester no longer consolidated its foreign subsidiaries: "The spread of war conditions during 1940 with resulting increased hazards and lack of information have so increased the difficulties of preparing a consolidated report which would fairly reflect the combined foreign and domestic assets and income, that the management concluded it would be unwise to present a consolidated report." International Harvester did list the investments in subsidiaries by countries. In 1960, all foreign subsidiaries were consolidated. In 1940, United Fruit removed the assets and liabilities of subsidiaries in the United Kingdom and Europe from the consolidated statements and showed them as the investment in Europe account on the balance sheet. A separate schedule was given for the assets and liabilities of these subsidiaries. The earnings of the European subsidiaries in the investment account were credited to deferred income in 1941. In 1954, the practice of consolidation returned. It is

interesting to note the very conservative philosophies followed by
these companies. With United States corporations more and more
involved with foreign subsidiaries, history might call for a contingency plan for accounting for foreign subsidiaries in troubled nations.

8 Reporting Surplus for Transactions Dealing
with the Company's Own Stock

Five of the 20 companies used their surplus accounts for transactions dealing with their own stock, excluding treasury stock. These
practices were caused by the combining of the earned surplus and
capital surplus accounts. One gets a greater appreciation for the
great stress placed on a tighter classification of the surplus account.
DuPont in 1928 used its surplus account for two transactions:
"surplus resulting from issue of 101,575 shares additional nonvoting
debenture stock" and "surplus appropriated in connection with issue of
149,392 shares of no par value common stock for Grasselli properties
and for additional capital required relative to the issuance of new $20
par value stock." In 1930, three more transactions dealing with
common stock were entered in the surplus account. Two occurred in
1931, one in 1933 and in 1937, three in 1939, and one in 1940. IBM in
1923 credited the declared capital and surplus account for the
"amount received from sale of 19,655 shares of ... capital stock
without par value" for $1.474 million. In 1925, the amount so
credited was $1.005 million. Kresge in 1921 credited $228,000 to
surplus for "proceeds from sale of common stock in excess of par." In
1930, "profit on sale of company's own capital stock held for
investment of $18,000" was included in the surplus account. Union
Oil deducted $90,000 from surplus for "Commission on sale of Capital
stock" in 1924. In 1925, $187,000 was credited for "premium on
capital stock sold to employees" and in 1926, $5,000 was debited for
"premium on employees' stock subscription cancelled." United Fruit
credited $38,000 to surplus in 1905 for "Premium on new issues of
capital stock." In 1911, $1.125 million was credited to surplus for
"premium received from sale of the company's capital stock issued in
payment for additional European investments." In 1912, a $0.731
million credit for "premiums of 100 percent on 7,306 shares issued
during the year in payment for property" and a $3.050 million credit
for "premium of 50 percent on 60,990 shares offered to stockholders
under company's circular of September 5, 1912" were placed in the
surplus account.

9 Charging Expenses and Losses to Capital Surplus

One of the companies utilized capital surplus for expense and
loss charges. (Refer to item #48 for write-downs and write-offs of

fixed assets to capital surplus.)   Calumet & Hecla utilized its
consolidated capital surplus in 1936 for a $671,000 charge for "re-
serve for retirement of workers." In 1938, there were two deductions
from consolidated capital surplus, one for $250,000 for "reserve for
exploratory work" and a second for $10,000 for "book value of mining
rights surrendered." In 1939, $400,000 was debited to capital surplus
for "reserve for exploratory work." In 1940, $140,000 was "reserved
for contingent federal taxes for prior years." In 1942, the capital
surplus account had a credit of $136,000 for "reserve for exploratory
work" and a debit for "inventory adjustment" of $118,000. Similar
activity took place in 1943, 1944, and 1945.

10 Offsetting of U.S. Treasury Notes against Tax Liability

Seven of the companies adopted the policy of offsetting U.S.
Treasury notes against federal income taxes payable. They were: #5
(1943-63), #7 (1949-65), #11 (1952-62), #17 (1951-55), #18 (1942-46),
#19 (1947-58), and #20 (1954-66).

11 Discussion of the Earned Surplus Account

Detailed discussions of the earned surplus account occurred in 4
of the companies.   Diamond International, in 1928, stressed "This
figure may or may not be usable surplus or surplus in fact, in case of
liquidation. It may represent a mere arithmetical difference between
assets and liabilities as stated on the books." International Harvester
transferred $66.138 million for surplus to capital in 1928, $84.551
million in 1944, and $63.683 million in 1947. The explanation offered
in 1944 was that:

> It has always been the policy of the company to
> retain in the business a portion of its earnings for the
> purpose of providing the additional capital which is re-
> quired from time to time for new and more efficient
> facilities, and for the healthy progress of the business
> with increased employment and better service to cus-
> tomers. The new plants and facilities which are an im-
> portant part of the company's post-war program, together
> with the necessary working capital, will require retention
> in the business of the accumulated earnings now in the
> surplus account. The Board of Directors feels that this
> fact should be reflected in the balance sheet by the
> transfer of the greater part of the surplus to the capital
> account.

Union Oil transferred $10 million from surplus to a general reserve
account in 1913. It wrote:

It has become evident to your Board of Directors that many stockholders misunderstood the nature of the surplus account as carried in former balance sheets, and supposed it to represent funds at any time for dividends. It has, therefore, been thought wise to take such reinvestments out of surplus account and list them as a reserve.

The company delineated its policy toward surplus as "to apportion to surplus account only so much earnings as have not been invested for capital purposes."

United Fruit wrote in 1948:

For many years the company has followed the policy of retaining a part of its earnings to finance new developments and provide improved facilities. Since the major portion of the earnings thus plowed back into the business has been invested in fixed assets, the Board of Directors, by resolution of December 13, 1948, transferred $81,500,328.74 from surplus to capital, increasing the capital stock account to $200,000,000. This action did not alter the number or value of shares of stock authorized or outstanding.

12 Reclassification of Surplus into Components

Five of the companies experienced a reclassification of surplus into its components. In 1934, Armour reclassified its $49.554 million of surplus into capital and paid-in surplus, $35.254 million; appropriated earned surplus, $4.911 million; unappropriated earned surplus, $9.388 million. DuPont yielded in 1952 to the Securities and Exchange Commission on the issue of segregation of surplus by establishing an earned surplus account, a paid-in surplus account, and a surplus arising from revaluation of security investments account. There was an unusual split between DuPont and its auditors in 1943 on this issue. DuPont's Committee on Audit wrote:

The Committee on Audit cannot accept the opinion of Arthur Andersen & Company as being conclusive for the reason that it believes that certain of the items comprising the Surplus Account are not susceptible of such a segregation except on the basis of arbitrary assumptions or interpretation, and that the company can have no assurance that at some later date the accuracy of the segregation may not be questioned and if found inaccurate the company might not be deemed to have published erroneous information which had served to mislead the stockholders and the investing public.

General Electric established a capital surplus account in 1945: $9.111 million was removed from earned surplus, as well as $8.415 million from the general reserve account, to the capital surplus account. IBM established separate accounts for capital stock and earned surplus in its 1934 balance sheet. Union Oil in 1933 reclassified its capital surplus into premium on sale of capital stock and appreciation of proven oil properties.

13 Valuation of Marketable Securities

There have been many valuation bases for marketable securities. (See Table 2, p. 72).

14 Examples of Discussion of Working Capital

Discussions about the working capital position were not unusual occurrences. Here are 7 examples from different companies of such discussions, showing that the item was an important part of financial reporting. Armour in 1924 noted an improvement in its working capital ratio from 2.62 to 1 at the end of 1923 to 3.33 to 1 at the end of 1924. Diamond International in its 1913 annual report included a schedule listing current and operating assets, current and deferred liabilities, and net working capital on a comparative basis for the last six years. In 1924, the company made this comment on its switch from the fixed assets first to the current assets first format: "The balance sheet...gives priority to current or liquid assets and current liabilities, subordinates the plant account to last place."

DuPont stressed its working capital position in 1907: "The working capital of the company, while at all times adequate, has been largely increased to care for our improved methods of raw materials. This working capital now almost equals the entire indebtedness of the company including all bonds outstanding." Hart, Schaffner & Marx stated in its 1930 annual report that the ratio of current assets to liabilities was 26 to 1. International Harvester disclosed a comparative schedule of working capital as of 12/31/1911 and 12/31/1910 in its 1911 annual report. Kresge in its 1938 annual report showed five-year comparative information on (1) excess of cash and government securities over current liabilities, (2) ratio of current assets to current liabilities, and (3) net working capital. Union Oil in its 1919 annual report disclosed a five-year comparison of current assets minus current liabilities. U.S. Rubber's auditors stressed in the Auditors' Certificate in the 1902 annual report the strength of the company's liquidity position: "And, that the quick assets including inventories of raw materials and manufactured goods on hand, exceeded all the liabilities of the United States Rubber Company and its subsidiary companies...to the extent of $7.736 million."

15 Write-up of Investments

Four companies wrote up their investment account. General Electric wrote up its securities held by $2.058 million in 1902. The explanation was that

> Due to the rapid growth of electric enterprises in all parts of the country, the value of the company's investments in stocks and bonds of local lighting and railway companies has greatly increased, particularly during the past year.

> No substantial change having been made in the book value of these securities since January of 1897 (a period of five years) the directors have now made a careful valuation of all the separate items of stocks and bonds remaining on hand at January 31, 1902.

DuPont began in 1923 its policy of writing-up its investment in General Motors stock. The account credited was surplus until 1952, when it became credited to surplus arising from revaluation of security investments. This policy ended in 1965. The amount of the write-ups until 1952 was $419.315 million and after 1952 was $438.354 million. Pullman wrote up the value of its investments for $1.151 million in 1898 and $0.816 million in 1899. United Fruit in 1918 credited surplus for $1.897 million for the appreciation of securities held by the Old Colony Trust Company as trustee.

TOPIC II
INCOME STATEMENT PRESENTATION
AND PHILOSOPHY

16 First Year of Income Statement

An income statement appeared in the first annual report studied for 12 of the 20 companies (see Table 3, p. 73). Two of these 12 companies, #3, Armour, and #13, Kresge, later dropped the income statement--Armour in 1920, resuming again in 1923 and Kresge in 1913, resuming again in 1926. The remaining 8 companies varied from 1896 to 1930 for first reporting an income statement. Number 17, Union Oil, dropped its income statement in 1911 and resumed it in 1912. Number 18, U.S. Rubber, dropped its income statement in 1919 and resumed again in 1931. It is evident that while the concept of income statement reporting was a well-established one even in the nineteenth century, a significant number of these companies just did not report income statements.

17 Comparative Income Statements

Only 5 of the companies presented comparative income statements at their first opportunity (see Table 3, p. 73). They were #6, DuPont, #12, International Harvester, #13, Kresge, #19, United Fruit, and #20, U.S. Steel. Since the first 4 of these companies later dropped this practice and then resumed it, only U.S. Steel has had a continuous reporting of comparative income statements. The remaining 15 companies took as late as 1966 to report comparative income statements, so it is evident that there must have been strong management resistance and/or disinterest to this reporting. The number of the 15 companies that also dropped their once adopted practice--#3, Armour, #5, Diamond International, #17, Union Oil, and #18, U.S. Rubber--also illustrated the ambivalence of management. This issue also shows the apparent impotence of the AIA in ARB #6, issued in April, 1940.

> The increasing use of the comparative statements in the annual reports of companies is a step in the right direction. The practice enhances the significance of the reports, and brings out more clearly the nature and trends of current changes affecting the enterprise. The use of statements in comparative form serves to increase the reader's grasp of the fact that the statements for a series of periods are far more significant than those for a single period--that the statements for one year are but one installment of what is essentially a continuous history.

> It is therefore recommended that the use of comparative statements be extended. In any one year it is ordinarily desirable that the balance sheet, the income statement and the surplus statement (the two latter being separate or combined) be given for the preceding as well as for the current year. (6)

These companies took some years after 1940 to issue or reissue comparative income statements: #1 (1954), #2 (1960), #3 (1947), #4 (1950), #5 (1949), #10 (1945), #11 (1955), #14 (1948), #16 (1966), #17 (1942), #18 (1944), and #19 (1956). This is evidence that the strength of the general acceptability of ARB's did not lead to immediate compliance. ARB's were authoritative to the extent of their general acceptability. (7)

18 Reporting the Revenue Figures in the Income Statement

Only 7 of the 20 companies reported their revenue figures on their first income statements studied (see Table 3, p. 73). They were #6, DuPont, 1907; #10, Hart, Schaffner & Marx, 1911; #12, International Harvester, 1907; #13, Kresge, 1912; #15, Pullman, 1875; #16, Quincy Mining, 1861; and #20, U.S. Steel, 1902. The first 4 of these companies later dropped and then resumed this disclosure practice, leaving only 3 companies with a continuous practice of disclosing the revenue figure on the income statement. The remaining 13 companies had varying amounts of time before the revenue figure was reported: #1, American Bank Note Company (1906), 1954; #2, American Ship Building Company (1900), 1960; #3, Armour (1910), 1937; #4, Calumet & Helca Mining (1884), 1917; #5,

Diamond International (1899), 1938; #7, Eastman Kodak (1902), 1935; #8, General Electric (1893), 1894; #9, General Motors (1911), 1933; #11, IBM (1911), 1936; #14, Nabisco (1899), 1945; #17, Union Oil (1903), 1934; #18, U.S. Rubber (1893), 1902; and #19, United Fruit (1900), 1956.   As with the first two income statement items management disclosure practices varied widely.

19 Dividends Deducted from Net Income

It was interesting to note that 19 of the 20 companies at one time or another deducted dividends paid from net income to get the "amount to transfer to surplus." They were: #1, 1906-16; #2, 1901-15 (preferred stock); #3, 1923-26 (preferred stock), 1928-29 (preferred stock), 1939-43 (preferred stock); #4, 1917-18; #5, 1907-22; #6, 1907-20, 1926-52 (preferred stock); #7, 1904-30, 1948-65; #8, 1893; #9, 1911-69 (preferred stock); #10, 1913-19 (preferred stock); #11, 1916-34; #12, 1907-12, 1927-29, 1962-69; #13, 1915-16; #14, 1926-30; #15, 1875-31; #17, 1909-11; #18, 1896-1901, 1919-20; #19, 1901-25; and #20, 1902-69.   It is evident that many managements have perceived dividends to be a component of the yearly addition to retained earnings than to be a distribution from the retained earnings account.   Perhaps some rethinking by accountants is needed about what management perceives a dividend to be, especially a dividend on preferred stock.

20 Income of Unconsolidated Subsidiaries

Item 7, Accounting for Subsidiaries in Turbulent Times, should be read along with this item, as there is some overlap. Nine of the companies mentioned the handling of the income of unconsolidated subsidiaries. Armour stated in 1949 that only dividends received in U.S. dollars from foreign subsidiaries were to be included in income. DuPont in 1919 made reference to the vast increase of undivided profits of unconsolidated subsidiaries: "In the past, the undistributed earnings on investment stocks shown in our balance sheet was not a considerable item, so that the usual practice of omitting reference to them was followed. This year, however, the amount has risen to such proportions as to be very material in measuring the earnings capacity of your company." The amount of 1919 undivided profits accruing to DuPont stockholders was $16.016 million. The amount per share was stated as $27.37. In 1926, the equity policy was made clearer by an income statement caption of income from operations, including DuPont's equity in earnings of controlled companies. DuPont wrote in 1944 that its "equity in undivided profits of controlled companies not wholly owned has increased since acquisition by a net amount of approximately $5.579 million which is not included in surplus." Kodak reported in 1932 that its not wholly owned investments had an equity value which "has been increased through earnings by $1.736 million, no part of which is reflected in the accounts."

General Electric took $750,000 in 1909 into the earnings part of its income statement for "surplus earnings of manufacturing and other companies," although the total of such earnings was $900,000. General Electric stated in its 1937 annual report that its investments in affiliated companies were adjusted yearly to reflect changes in the net worth of such companies. This adjustment was credited to surplus every year until 1956, when substantially owned domestic subsidiaries were consolidated. Also, the investment accounts for foreign nonconsolidated subsidiaries were to remain at cost, and hence, would no longer be adjusted for changes in their retained earnings. General Motors in 1933 adopted a policy of including in its income statement the "equity in the undivided profits or losses of subsidiary and affiliated companies, not consolidated." Hart, Schaffner & Marx began its policy of separate reporting of the parent and subsidiary operations in its 1931 income statement. In 1937, for example, it noted that while reported profit for subsidiaries on the income statement was $77,000, "The parent company's equity in the net operating profits of all of its subsidiary and affiliated companies for the year was $102,000." This policy continued until 1943 when the subsidiaries were consolidated with the parent.

IBM in its 1926 annual report stated that the amount of $0.237 million for "undistributed surplus and profit of foreign subsidiaries" was added to the cost of the investment account entitled "Securities of and advances to other companies, including foreign subsidiaries." IBM in 1954 reported income for its foreign subsidiary, the IBM World Trade Corporation, as dividends were received, rather than on the basis of the net earnings of subsidiaries, which had been followed since 1926. However, for the years 1935-53, IBM had debited the investment account and credited the reserve for foreign investments account for profits. IBM readopted the basis of the net earnings of the subsidiary in 1961.

International Harvester in 1949 disclosed a schedule of the areas in which foreign subsidiaries were located and listed the cost of such investments of $85.143 million and its equity of $151.771 million as well as a company equity in 1949 earnings of $17.192 million and cash dividends of $11.482 million. In 1960 all foreign subsidiaries were consolidated and the International Harvester Credit Corporation was recorded on the equity method.

Union Oil noted in 1914 the amount of its proportion of the net profits of controlled companies in a note to the income statement.

This notation said that the amount was included in the computation of profit. This disclosure policy continued until 1923 and was readopted in 1934. In 1936, the equity in net earnings of controlled companies of $73,000, was classified as a non-operating income item on the revamped income statement. Union Oil stated in 1947 that it continued to value its unconsolidated subsidiaries with wasting assets on the equity basis but other unconsolidated subsidiaries were now carried at cost, which was stated as being $747,000 lower than equity. In 1956, investment in capital stocks of majority owned companies was stated on the cost basis with the equity amount shown parenthetically. In 1957, no parenthetical notation of equity value was made.

U.S. Rubber in 1896 noted that there was $1.912 million of earnings on investments which had not yet been paid into the treasury of the parent. In 1898, two notations--"the manufacturing companies in which this company has investments earned net for the year, in excess of dividends paid," for $254,000, and "the undivided earnings in the treasuries of such companies are now" $2.049 million-- appeared under the income statement. In 1899, the amounts were $439,000 and $2.488 million, respectively. Only the undivided earnings amount of $2.689 million was shown in the 1900 income statement and $1.175 million was shown for "the undivided earnings in the treasuries of the manufacturing companies in which this company has investments, after charging off depreciation" in 1901. In 1910, once again reference was made to undivided earnings of unconsolidated holdings. The notation was "should we add to these net profits the company's in which it is a stockholder, which are not included in the consolidated statement, the profits for the year would be about $7.235 million." U.S. Rubber in 1932 reported in the notes to the balance sheet section that the net worth of securities of controlled companies was $4.590 million, compared to the company's book value of such securities of $3.767 million. The increase in net worth for the year was $129,000.

United Fruit in 1900 reported earnings of subsidiaries as a caption in the income statement. It reported in 1941 that income earned by its United Kingdom and Continental European subsidiaries, which had been classified as an investment since 1939 rather than being consolidated, was being credited to a deferred income account. This policy apparently ceased in 1949.

There is no doubt that uniformity was not present in these cases. Whether uniformity is possible or even desirable is an important question to face, especially in the light of the previous discussion in Item #7.

21 Examples of the Use of Noncurrent
Liability Reserve Accounts

The breakdown of the number of different noncurrent reserves in the liability part of the balance sheet by company showed: #1 (8), #2 (18), #3 (9), #4 (3), #6 (5), #7 (9), #8 (7), #9 (12), #10 (2), #11 (10), #12 (10), #13 (7), #14 (7), #15 (14), #16 (15), #17 (10), #18 (14), #19 (14), and #20 (11). An analysis of the transactions with these accounts was too voluminous to attempt in this study. However, it is possible to relate some examples of companies which made special note of their use of noncurrent liability reserve accounts. With this long list and these few examples, one can understand the stress placed by the American Institute of Accountants (AIA) in ARB #26 and ARB #28.

ARB #26,   *Accounting for the Use of Special War Reserves,* called in 1946 for limits on the use of special wartime reserves accounts:

> 7.   In the opinion of the committee costs and losses which may arise from such causes as: (a) strikes occurring after the resumption of peacetime operations; (b) failure to achieve full peacetime production because of material or other shortages; (c) failure to make profits on peacetime products because of the limitations of price ceilings or because of the lack of full production; and (d) inventory losses on peacetime products from future deflationary price adjustments, should be considered proper charges to peacetime revenues and hence, in general, such items are not considered appropriate charges to reserves created for expenses, costs or losses allocable to the income of the war period. (8)

ARB #28, *Accounting Treatment of General Purpose Contingency Reserves,* called in 1948 for tight restrictions on the use of contingency reserves.

> 3.   When a reserve is provided by a charge to income, the amount recorded as net income for the period is correspondingly reduced. If the provision is not properly chargeable to current revenues, net income for the period is understated by the amount of the provision. If such a reserve should then be used to relieve the income of subsequent periods of charges that would otherwise be made there-against, the income of such subsequent periods would be thereby overstated. When a reserve is used

in this manner, profit for a given period may be significantly increased or decreased by mere whim. When this practice is followed the integrity of financial statements is impaired and they tend to be misleading and of doubtful value. The committee is therefore of the opinion that general contingency reserves, such as those created
(a) for general undetermined contingencies, or
(b) for a wide variety of indefinite possible future losses, or
(c) without any specific purpose reasonably related to the operations for the current period, or
(d) in amounts not determined on the basis of any reasonable estimates of costs or losses,
are of such a nature that charges or credits relating to such reserves should not enter into the determination of net income. (9)

DuPont in 1920 wrote down inventory for $10.342 million to a previously created reserve for contingencies. In 1921, the amount written off to this reserve was $8.681 million. In 1942, DuPont stated its World War II reserve policy:

In 1942, net income is after reversion thereto of $5,303,874, representing provision for taxes on income in prior years in excess of liability (page 9), and after setting aside $5,000,000 to provide additional contingent reserve for possible shrinkage in inventory values and other possible costs and expenses which may be occasioned by the war period but which cannot now be determined definitely. The contingent reserve now totals $25,000,-000, provision of $10,000,000 having been made in each of the years 1940 and 1941.

Kodak in 1904 used its reserve for the repository of items of gain or loss.

During the year a profit of $125,322.97 accrued to the company upon the realization of certain properties previously acquired on very favorable terms through one of the subsidiary companies. This profit being of an extraordinary character, and incident to a capital purchase, it has been regarded as available for capital purposes only, and placed to the credit of a special reserve account, and is not included in the earnings.

Kodak started in 1931 to disclose the happenings in the reserve for contingencies account. This disclosure continued until 1949. A sample of this disclosure is the following excerpt from the 1934 annual report, in which the reserve account increased by $3.5 million.

Net gain on delivery of silver bullion to United States Assay Office		$1,550,045.60
Increase in dollar value of net current assets of foreign subsidiary companies, consolidated, to exchange rates at close of year		624,293.83
Restoring to reserves recovery in market value of securities (previously appropriated therefrom)		726,667.43
Unemployment-reserve fund included in accounts payable on the balance sheet in 1933 ($291,068.03) now transferred to reserves, and net additions to such fund ($102,557.88) charged to operations in 1934		393,625.91
Inventory and other reserves provided in prior years and no longer required		142,864.11
Other credits	$121,784.56	
Less: Other charges	56,108.55	65,676.01
		$3,503,172.89

General Motors began in 1939 its policy of deductions from the special contingency reserve provided in view of disturbed conditions abroad. The amounts so charged were $10 million in 1939, $16.599 million in 1941, $23.986 million in 1942, and $35.467 million in 1943. Hart, Schaffner & Marx in 1930 wrote off $250,000 to the "reserve for contingencies" for "charges in respect of prior years." In 1942, the company charged $150,000 for contingencies as a component of the profit of the parent company. In 1943, $200,000, and in 1944, $100,000 were charged as extraordinary items on the respective income statements.

International Harvester in 1909 discussed its contingency reserve policy:

Last year the reserve for deferred profits on forward sales amounted to $750,000, and was deducted from the receivables in the balance sheet, as explained in 1908 Annual Report. Assuming a continuance of present credit methods and the same proportion of forward sales, it is proposed to build up this reserve to a maximum of $2,500,000; and it has been decided to classify it with the other reserves in the 1909 balance sheet under the heading contingent. Theoretically and technically, a profit is earned when the sale is made; but when the actual realization of the profit on certain sales is deferred a considerable time beyond the close of the fiscal year, it is obviously a conservative and sensible policy to establish a contingent reserve to meet this condition inherent in the business. This policy prevents the misleading transfer of book earnings to surplus, where a long period of time elapses between the date of the sale and the realization of the profit in cash.

```
Balance of contingent reserve at
   December 31, 1908                    $   750,000.00
   Add:
      Provision for 1909                   500,000.00
   Balance at Dec. 31, 1909             $1,250,000.00
```

The company transferred its net profit for 1915 of $1.620 million to the contingent reserve (European war losses, etc.). In 1916, the net profit of $3.037 million was also carried to the contingent reserve for exchange and war losses. In 1917, the net loss of $.351 million was charged to the contingent reserve. In 1928, the company collected $2.058 million of its post-war losses and credited this amount to its pension reserve.

Nabisco noted in 1932 that earnings were not charged for strike expenses of $721,000, which was debited to the insurance and contingent reserve. U.S. Rubber in 1912 noted that the "reserve for contingencies, amounting to $500,000 shown in the consolidated balance sheet of March 31, 1911, was used for reduction in value of manufacturing good for which purpose it was set up."

22 Transactions in Company's Own Stock

One company used the income statement for transactions of its own stock. Quincy Mining in 1906 added $700,000 to business profit for "Receivables from 10,000 shares increased capital stock." In 1928, two types of capital stock transactions appeared on the income statement. One was $500,000 from the sale of Treasury stock. The other was $893,000 for subscribed capital stock. In 1930, $649,000 was included for the new stock issue of that year.

TOPIC III
EARNED SURPLUS
AND EXTRAORDINARY ITEMS

23 Use of Earned Surplus for Items of Income
and Expense and of Gain and Loss

The allegations of the followers of the "all-inclusive" school stated in ARB #32, *Income and Earned Surplus,* remain as harsh as any judgment made by accountants about managerial instincts.

7. Proponents of the "all-inclusive" type of income statement insist that annual income statements taken for the life of an enterprise should, when added together, represent total net income. They emphasize the dangers of possible manipulation of annual earnings if material extraordinary items may be omitted in the determination of income. They also assert that, over a period of years, charges resulting from extraordinary events tend to exceed the credits, and their omission has the effect of indicating a greater earning · performance than the corporation actually has exhibited. They insist that an income statement including all income charges or credits arising during the year is simple to prepare, is easy to understand, and is not subject to variations resulting from the different judgments that may be applied in the treatment of individual items. They argue that when judgment is allowed to enter the picture with respect to

the inclusion or exclusion of special items, material differences in the treatment of borderline cases will develop and that there is danger that the use of "distortion" as a criterion may be a means of rationalizing the normalization of earnings. With full disclosure of the nature of any special or extraordinary items, this group believes the user of the financial statements can make his own additions or deductions more effectively than can the management or the independent accountant. (10)

If one were to assume that abuse by management would consist of an overwhelming difference between the dollar amount of debits and the dollar amount of credits to the earned surplus account, he should be surprised by Table 4 (p. 74). Seven of the 20 companies had a greater dollar amount of credits than debits. The remaining 13 companies had ratios of dollar amount of debits to credits as shown in Table 5 (p. 75).

Another test for the abuse assumption is a comparison of the number of debits to the number of credits. Six of these companies had more credit items than debit items. The remainder had those listed in Table 6 (p. 76).

The companies with a ratio of 2 to 1 or over in either or both of these tests is listed in Table 7 (p. 77).

A judgment as to perceived abuse of the surplus account rests upon an analysis of the actual entries, of the use of extraordinary items on the income statement, of the dollar totals of the surplus entries, and of the number of the debit and credit entries. The writer is of the opinion that companies #3, #9, #15, #18, and #19 could be perceived as possible abusers of the surplus account. However, the total dollar amounts of debit and credit entries cast doubts as to a general castigation of management on this issue.

24 Extraordinary Items on Income Statements

Another allegation about management behavior concerns the possibility of abuses concerning the classification of extraordinary items on the income statement. It is stated in APB (Accounting Principles Board) Opinion #9.

14. Proponents of this position believe that the aggregate of such periodic net incomes, over the life of an enterprise, constitutes total net income, and that this is the only fair and complete method of reporting the results of operations of the entity. They believe that extra-ordinary items and prior period adjustments are part of

the earnings history of an entity and that omission of such items from periodic statements of income increases the possibility that these items will be overlooked in a review of operating results for a period of years. They also stress the dangers of possible manipulation of annual earnings figures if such items may be omitted from the determination of net income. They believe that a statement of income including all such items is easy to understand and less subject to variations resulting from different judgments. They feel that, when judgment is allowed to determine whether to include or exclude particular items or adjustments, significant differences develop in the treatment of borderline cases and that there is a danger that the use of "extraordinary" as a criterion may be a means of equalizing income. Advocates of this theory believe that full disclosure in the income statement of the nature of any extraordinary items or prior period adjustments during each period will enable the user of a statement of income to make his own assessment of the importance of the items and their effects on operating results. (11)

The findings on the issue of the use of extraordinary items on the income statement is somewhat more clear cut than the previous issue. Five of the companies had a greater amount of dollar credits than dollar debits. The remainder had those listed in Table 8 (p. 77).

Four of the companies either had more credit entries than debit entries or had the same number of debits and credits. The remainder had those listed in Table 9 (p. 78).

The companies with a ratio of 2 to 1 or over in either or both of these tests are listed in Table 10 (p. 79).

The writer is of the judgment that companies #1, #2, #3, #10, #11, #16, #18, and #19 were probably abusive of the extraordinary item freedom. The sample size of 20 companies and the overall ratio of 1.35 to 1 for the total $ debits to $ credits are factors which make unwarranted a general castigation of management, especially in light of the fact that conservatism tends to encourage the writingdown of assets.

TOPIC IV
DEPRECIATION

25 First Mention of Depreciation

Nine of the companies mentioned depreciation as being an expense in their first annual reports studied, although the amount of depreciation might not have been included as a separate item in the income statement (see Table 11, p. 80). (Item 39 discusses the separate disclosure on the income statement.) Of the remaining 11 companies, only the 3 earliest companies had a lag of over 3 years before depreciation was mentioned.

26 Year the Method of Depreciation First Disclosed

While there was obviously a general acceptance of the notion of depreciation, the policy of disclosing the method of depreciation in the annual report was much later in gaining acceptability, as can be noted from an examination of Table 11 (p. 80).

27 Methods of Depreciation

Because of the lateness of the companies' disclosures of their methods of depreciation, this item is not as informative as it could have been (see Table 11, p. 80). It does show that 8 of the companies have placed great stress on their taxation method of depreciation:

#1, #4, #10, #12, #13, #14, #16, and #20. (This excludes wartime depreciation acceptance of taxation methods.) Pullman (#15) stated in 1937 it was following the ICC (Interstate Commerce Commission) method for depreciation and U.S. Rubber (#18) in 1934 said it was following trade policy in its depreciation policy. Twelve of the companies adopted an accelerated depreciation method (ACC or SYD): #5, #6, #7, #8, #9, #10, #11, #12, #14, #15, #17, and #20. However, 6 of these companies--#5, #12, #14, #15, #17, and #20- later reverted to the straight line (SL) approach. In 1960, Calumet & Hecla (#4) stated that its idle mine properties were depreciated on estimated deterioration rates.

28 Placement of the "Reserve for Depreciation"

There was a long and slow movement to the contra asset placement of the "reserve for depreciation." As one can note from Table 11 (p. 80). there also was a lag before any mention on the balance sheet of the "reserve for depreciation" account was even made. The last of the companies to switch to the contra asset placement was DuPont in 1965. It wrote:

> In prior reports to stockholders, the company has followed a consistent practice of showing its reserve for depreciation and obsolescence of plants and properties on the liability side of its consolidated balance sheet. However, in financial statements filed with the Securities and Exchange Commission this reserve has been shown as a deduction from plants and properties on the asset side of the balance sheet, as required by the commission. Since this reserve includes substantial amounts to protect against technical obsolescence, which is a factor of major importance in the chemical industry, the company views it more a contingency reserve than a valuation reserve, and therefore feels that in principle the reserve should be shown on the liability side of the balance sheet. Nevertheless, in view of a recent amendment made to the proxy rules under the Securities Exchange Act we have, beginning with this 1965 report to stockholders, transferred this reserve to the asset side of the balance sheet as a deduction from plants and properties.

29 Dropping Depreciation Once Instituted

Four of the companies failed to depreciate after a policy of yearly depreciation had commenced. American Ship Building apparently did not deduct an amount for depreciation from 1910 through

1915. For these years, while the compilation of the amount transferred to surplus for the year noted that its beginning figure was
earnings before deducting maintenance and depreciation, the deduction caption was entitled maintenance. Diamond International
reported no depreciation expense in 1906. U.S. Rubber did not charge
depreciation from 1902 through 1908. It was stated in the Auditors'
Certificate for 1902 that "In lieu of depreciation for the year all
betterments and improvements to the plants of the companies have
been charged to expense." In 1909, depreciation was again charged to
surplus. The treasurer wrote, "In view of these conditions (general
commercial depreciation) this has been deemed by your directors a
proper time to make a substantial charge to depreciation against
properties, plant accounts and securities owned and we have made a
charge against surplus account of $1.355 million." United Fruit
charged amounts expended for betterments, which were stated to be
in effect a provision for depreciation, against current operations from
1904 through 1910.

30 Evaluation by Management and/or Auditors of the
Amount of Depreciation

Thirteen of the 20 companies and/or their auditors utilized
terms like "adequate" and "liberal" to describe depreciation. One
company, U.S. Rubber (#18), had its depreciation described in a
negative manner (see Table 12, p. 82).

31 Effects on Depreciation of the Rising Price Level
after World War II

Nine of the 20 companies mentioned and/or acted on the rapidly
changing price level after World War II. American Bank Note made
this reference in 1948 to replacement cost depreciation:

> While the results of the year's operations were
> gratifying, it seems appropriate to mention that they do
> not take account of the marked increase in the re-
> placement cost of the fixed assets utilized in producing
> them. As in the past, depreciation charges were made on
> the basis of the original book value of such assets, which
> accords with generally accepted accounting practice and
> Bureau of Internal Revenue regulations. A recent study of
> the fixed assets of the company, exclusive of those of the
> subsidiaries, indicates, however, that, if depreciation had
> been accrued on the basis of current replacement cost, it
> would have resulted in a substantial additional charge
> against current income.

Diamond International included in its 1948 annual report a section entitled "Are Business Profits Really as High as They Appear":

> Another important qualification of reported profit arises from the method of computing depreciation of physical assets. The annual charge for depreciation is based on original cost and not replacement value. Fully depreciated assets which must be replaced now cost substantially in excess of their original cost. Furthermore, rapidly advancing technological developments may cause obsolescence of plants and equipment in far less time than generally allowed by tax authorities in establishing depreciation rates.

DuPont in 1947 took the step of adjusting its depreciation for the changing price level:

> Construction costs have more than doubled since 1939 and are continuing to increase. The index of construction costs published by the Engineering News-Record indicates that such costs have increased, on the average, about 73 percent over the 1939 levels. This index, when adjusted for factors currently handicapping field construction as compared with pre-war performance, shows that the aggregate actual costs of new plants erected and equipped today are more than twice those of 1939. The experience of the DuPont Company closely parallels this adjusted index.

> In view of these conditions, as stated in the first Quarterly Report to Stockholders for 1947, beginning January 1, 1947 the company is providing a reserve in anticipation of an eventual reduction in the level of overall construction costs upon the readjustment of these abnormalities. Accordingly, in the year 1947, $20,900,000 was set aside out of earnings for such a reserve, which amount is equivalent to approximately 20 percent of the construction expenditures during the year for plant extensions. This "excess construction cost" may be regarded as a penalty incurred by the company in order to serve its customers and secure earnings from the new capacities earlier than would have been the case had the projects been deferred.

In 1948, DuPont yielded to its auditors, the American Institute of Accountants, and the Securities and Exchange Commission on this issue but, at the same time, adopted an accelerated depreciation method which added $17.915 million to depreciation expense.

The company is well aware of the many problems involved in this situation and had considered the various views that have been expressed. In as much as none of these views has yet become generally accepted no change has been made in our established method. However, this should be made clear: our earnings are being determined and reported under conventional accounting practices. Therefore, they are much greater than they would be if put on a basis which stated all costs in terms of current prices. So long as this situation continues, the replacement of plant and equipment at current price levels will make it necessary to supplement the provision for depreciation by use of a substantial portion of retained earnings.

General Electric did not adopt the philosophy of replacement cost depreciation and explained its decision:

Many economists, professional accountants and others, realizing the seriousness of the problems created by a continuing decline in the purchasing power of the dollar, recently have given very careful consideration to the question of the adequacy of funds set aside by business concerns for the replacement of plant and equipment facilities. Certain groups have stated that they are disturbed by the apparent general lack of awareness of the fact that if a business is to survive it must maintain the productivity of its assets by reinvesting a substantial portion of its earnings. To insure that adequate replacement funds are available, some authorities have suggested that fundamental changes be made in the basis of accounting for depreciation.

General Electric's management has also given this matter careful consideration and has decided to continue to base depreciation charges on the original cost of plant and equipment, which method is recommended by the public accounting profession. The company has retained a substantial portion of its earnings in recent years and has consistently followed a conservative depreciation policy-- as indicated by the fact that the net plant value at the close of 1948 was less than the cost of additions during the past three years and less than seven times the amount of depreciation charged against income during the year under review.

Nabisco transferred $6 million from earnings to a special reserve for plant additions in 1947. It was explained thus:

The purchasing power of the dollars derived from current earnings is substantially less than was that of an equivalent sum resulting from pre-war earnings. Funds provided by depreciation provisions computed on cost (which remains the traditionally accepted basis upon which to compute such depreciation provisions) are inadequate, under prevailing conditions, to finance replacements of buildings, machinery and equipment. Accordingly, it is necessary to supplement such funds by retaining additional amounts of earnings in the business.

Union Oil included this comment in its 1947 annual report:

As a result of these factors, Union Oil Company made an apparently large profit for the year. But this profit must be realistically evaluated in the light of today's inflation. For, under accepted accounting principles and existing tax regulations, the amount the company can set aside before taxes for replacement of properties and facilities is based upon the original cost of these facilities, which bears little or no relationship to actual replacement costs under today's inflationary conditions.

Actually, drilling, material and construction costs are at least double pre-war levels. For instance, if we assume that increases have averaged only 50 percent and adjust the provision for replacements accordingly, the profit for the year, after preferred dividends, would be around 5 percent of our total revenue, instead of the recorded 10 1/2 percent.

United Fruit appropriated $7 million from net income because of the changing price level of fixed assets:

The post-war expansion program is progressing satisfactorily and during 1947, $33,817,335.49 was spent for additions to fixed assets of which $6,895,168.80 was for steamships. To take care of renewals and replacements of and improvements to existing properties and to provide further funds for the completion of the expansion program, $22,484,951.55 has been appropriated for capital expenditures during 1948; unexpected balances of previously authorized appropriations to be carried over to 1948 amounted to $18,691,186.76 making a total of $41,176,138.31 authorized for 1948. These large expenditures are being made at price levels for material and labor which are considerably in excess of pre-war costs and your directors have considered it advisable to set aside as an appropriation from 1947 net income the amount of $7,000,000 as a reserve for what is considered to be the abnormal construction costs.

In 1948, an additional $7 million was so charged to the income statement.

U.S. Steel adopted replacement cost depreciation in 1947 and, hence, added $26.3 million to cover replacement cost to the wear and facilities section of the income statement. Its explanation is as fine a one ever read by this writer.

Long Term Inventories--Believing that the same principle of recording the cost of short term inventories consumed (wear and exhaustion) of machinery, plants and mines, U.S. Steel in 1947 increased its provision for wear and exhaustion from $87.7 million based on original cost to $114.0 million, or by 30 percent. This was a step toward stating wear and exhaustion in an amount which will recover in current dollars of diminished buying power the same purchasing power as the original expenditure.

If a business is to continue, it is necessary to recover the purchasing power of sums originally invested in tools so that they may be replaced as they wear out. Therefore, this added amount is carried as a reserve for replacement of properties. It is a simple truth that to buy similar tools of production takes many more dollars today than formerly; to count as profits, rather than as cost, the added sums required merely to sustain production is to retreat from reality into self-deception.

The 30 percent increase in the provision for wear and exhaustion was determined partly through study of construction cost index numbers. Although it is materially less than the experienced cost increase in replacing worn out facilities, it was deemed appropriate in view of the newness of the application of this principle to the costing of wear and exhaustion. The use of index numbers for cost purposes gained recognition early in 1947 in a Tax Court decision in Hutzler Brothers Company, Petitioner v. Commissioner of Internal Revenue, Respondent. Although this case deals only with costing short term inventories, the principles set forth are just as applicable to costing the wear and exhaustion of long term inventories.

While awaiting accounting and tax acceptance, U.S. Steel believed that it was prudent for it to give some recognition to these increased replacement costs rather than to sit idly by and witness the unwitting liquidation of its business should inadequate recording of costs result in insufficient resources to supply the tools required for sustained production.

U.S. Steel dropped its notion of replacement cost depreciation in 1948 but adopted a version of accelerated depreciation in that year.

32 Emergency Write-off Provisions of
World War II and the Korean Conflict

Eight of the 20 companies utilized the Emergency Write-off Provivsions of World War II and 6 did for the Korean conflict (see Table 13, p. 82).

33 Notations of Major Write-downs of Fixed
Assets on Depreciation

Five of the 20 companies noted the effect major write-downs of fixed assets would have on the reduction of subsequent depreciation expense. The companies were Armour in 1934, General Motors in 1933, Pullman in 1932, United Fruit in 1932, and U.S. Steel in 1935. For example, U.S. Steel wrote, "It follows that future depreciation allowances should not be made therefore in reporting consolidated net income.   This reduction in annual depreciation allowances will, however, be offset, in part at least, by increased allowances in calculated future depreciation charges which will result from the revised depreciation rates indicated by the analysis above mentioned."

34 Adjustments of Depreciation Due
to Tax Rulings

Three of the companies noted adjustments to depreciation because of the desire to agree with tax rulings. American Bank Note wrote in 1934 that

In compliance with the regulations of the Internal Revenue Department the company's engineers have just completed estimates as to the future life of the various units of machinery and equipment carried in the accounts as of December 31, 1934. On this basis the annual provisions for depreciation beginning with January 1, 1935 will be increased by approximately $50,000 to provide for depreciation of these properties over the period of the remaining life as so determined.

Kresge in 1935 credited the surplus account for $2.043 million for "adjustment of properties and reserves for depreciation for the four years ending December 31, 1934, to basis used for computing amended income tax." In 1950, another credit to surplus for $604,000 resulted from an agreement with the Treasury Department. U.S. Steel decided in 1944 to follow the method "agreed upon by the Bureau of Internal Revenue for tax purposes," after an assessment for additional federal income taxes for excess depreciation.

35 Relationship between Lower Activity and Depreciation

Four companies commented on the relationship between a lower level of activity and a lower amount of depreciation expense. They were Armour in 1934, American Bank Note in 1934, International Harvester in 1932, and U.S. Steel in 1908, 1911, and 1914. For instance, American Bank Note wrote in 1934:

> Provision has been made for depreciation on buildings, machinery, tools and equipment at rates believed to be adequate. In continuance of the policy adopted by the company in 1931, the provision for depreciation of machinery and motors at certain plants has been computed on percentages which were somewhat less than the basic rates, the operations at the plants having been considerably below normal.

36 Special Charges for Depreciation

Seven of the companies utilized the special charge approach for depreciation. Calumet & Hecla in 1952 stated that "Depletion for both years included abnormal charges in connection with several high cost mines which are rapidly approaching exhaustion." Diamond International wrote in 1903 that "We have also thought it wise to depreciate and readjust the values of our foreign and domestic properties in these times of our prosperity." Diamond International made a special charge for depreciation of $150,000 from 1909 through 1916. In 1917, the amount of the special charge was $180,000. DuPont reported in 1915 there was a heavy charge for amortization of new facilities built because of wartime demand. General Electric in 1918 took an additional amount of depreciation because of wartime exigencies, which forced a quick building of plants without adequate manufacturing equipment available and at a much higher cost.

General Motors in 1947 adopted this depreciation policy for buildings:

> With respect to buildings, it has not, of course, been possible to identify potential extraordinary obsolescence

with any particular building or buildings. However, since increased risks of obsolescence are the result of the program undertaken to meet the postwar demand for General Motors products, the policy has been adopted of making annual provisions for such additional potential obsolescence based on a percentage of the gross value of postwar building additions. As mentioned in the Third Quarter Report to Stockholders, beginning as of January 1, 1947 provision has been made for extraordinary obsolescence of buildings. For the year 1947, the first year of substantial publication with the new facilities, this provision amounted to $14,781,664.

The amount of $14.927 million was deducted in 1947 for extraordinary obsolescence of buildings, compared to $13.492 million in 1948 and $17.387 million in 1950. Pullman in 1912 had a special depreciation account entitled "reserve for further depreciation on cars, in general" for $2 million. Pullman in 1924 stated that "The present day cost of cars exceeds the amount available through depreciation accumulated on the low priced cars now being retired, and an appropriation of $1 million has been made to care for the excess cost involved in replacing the retired units." This policy was continued in 1925 and 1926.

United Fruit in 1911 made a special charge to surplus for $588,000 for depreciation on cultivations and transportation equipment in its tropical properties. This policy continued until 1918. U.S. Steel use of this policy was summarized in a schedule in 1919, which noted that $182.093 million had been appropriated and applied in retirement through sinking funds of U.S. Steel corporation bonds (a charge U.S. Steel regarded as an adjustment of depreciation), that $207.709 million was applied to direct property purchases, and $118.502 million was applied to surplus. U.S. Steel also deducted $29.785 million in 1917, $40 million in 1918, $38.298 million in 1919, and $27 million in 1920 from the condensed general profit and loss account for an "allowance for estimated proportion of extraordinary cost of facilities installed by reason of war effort." In 1918, $12.215 million was also deducted in the income account for this purpose. (U.S. Steel presented its income computation in two statements-- condensed general profit and loss account and the income account.)

37 Explanations (or Defenses) of Depreciation Policies

Five of the companies presented explanations (or defenses) of their depreciation policies. Diamond International wrote in 1924:

Business and operating conditions that developed

early in the post-war period of readjustment definitely
indicated that the deductions from earnings for depreciation, amortization, supersession and obsolescence were
inadequate for the war years, which, while showing large
volume of business and relative high earnings, were,
nevertheless, periods of extraordinary changes, forced
expansion and unusual commitments. Because of (1) the
highly competitive nature of your company's business and
(2) the economic desirability of importing the foreign type
of "strike on box" match, rather than continue to
manufacture in quantity in domestic plants--built and
equipped at high cost to supply the national demand during
the war--sound, conservative accounting has suggested
that the property and plant account be written down
substantially during the years 1921-1924 inclusive--partly
by the application of previously accrued reserves, such as
the general reserve--to make up for the apparent insuf-
ficiency of certain depreciation and associated amortization deduction of the war years and to place your
company in a favorable position to cope with competition
in all its phases.

DuPont in 1926 explained its depreciation policy:

Your company's policy with respect to depreciation
is believed to be a conservative one. The rates employed
for the different industries and subdivisions of property
are reviewed regularly, with the view of making revisions
when warranted. Such rates vary from 3 percent per
annum in some of the older well-established lines to as
high as 20 percent as applied to special equipment in some
of the newer industries.

The main purpose for which your company's depreciation reserves are created is to provide for obsolescence of permanent assets, which in the chemical
industry is an important factor, as more fully described
herein under "research." Maintenance repairs and replacements are charged to operations as they occur.

In 1896, General Electric indicated it used depreciation as a
method to achieve replacement value accounting. "In addition large
reductions have been made at the close of each fiscal year, for the
purpose of writing this account to replacement value." In 1926,
General Electric gave this very informative insight into its depreciation policy:

The tendency in modern industry is for factories to
increase in size and in specialization. The value of a

manufacturing building lies very largely in its use for the purpose for which it was designed. Buildings are more and more being designed for the production of a particular thing. Processes are also being constantly improved by concentration of production, by progressive assembly, and by special machinery. This results frequently in scrapping machinery and tools which are not worn out and in rendering buildings less well adapted to the job for which they were designed. The type of construction, arrangement of space, headroom clearances and floor load capacity may well render a building undesirable for use long before the expiration of its normal life.

. . .

Normal depreciation on buildings and equipment is based upon the estimated average effective life of each unit. It does not take into consideration the rapid obsolescence of plants and machinery in a rapidly developing industry like ours. The value of a plant, therefore, cannot safely be determined by first cost nor by appraisal on the basis of reproduction cost less normal depreciation.

It is for these reasons that your company has followed the policy of providing a general plant reserve in excess of normal depreciation rates, so as to enable it to take promptly out of service buildings or equipment which, although not worn out physically, are inefficient and uneconomical. Failure to provide such a reserve would make the management much slower to abandon inefficient buildings and machinery, and would make the company less able to meet new conditions and, therefore, less effective in economical production and in competition.

It wrote in 1931 that

Annual reports of the past, notably those for 1926 and 1928, have outlined a policy of plant depreciation and valuation. Depreciation goes on whether plant is used to capacity or partially idle. Very little of the plant, except the land on which it is located, remains until used up or worn out; more is replaced by buildings and equipment which are superior or better adapted to the job to be done. A manufacturing organization's progress may be measured to some extent by the rapidity of its change in plant, bringing about better methods, improved quality of products, and lower costs. With lower costs come reduced selling prices, followed by increased business, and a greater use of plant. When plant value is low on the books, management is more responsive to the introduction of new methods and better tools.

International Harvester in 1907 had a charge of $1 million on the income statement. The explanation was that "The annual appropriation from earnings for depreciation and extinguishment reserves constitute the necessary provision for the impairment and consumption of plant assets utilized in the output of the product and should eventually prove sufficient to reproduce the properties as their replacement becomes necessary. Depreciation on plant property has been calculated at rates established by recognized authorities."

Union Oil wrote in 1914 that its depreciation policy "has been to make increasing larger apportionments to the reserve for depreciation and exhaustion, so that the net value at which the various assets are carried on the books will be realizable amounts."

38 Amount of Accumulated Depreciation
(Reserve for Depreciation)
as a Contra Asset

The range of years of the disclosure of the amount of the accumulated depreciation (or reserve for depreciation) account as a contra asset account was from 1899 to 1965 (see Table 14, Col. A, p. 83). Six of the companies had a lag between adopting the contra asset procedure and the disclosure of the amount of the contra asset account; #2 adopted in 1927 and disclosed in 1921, #7 adopted in 1914 and disclosed in 1930, #8 adopted in 1894 and disclosed in 1917, #9 adopted in 1914 and disclosed in 1918, #13 adopted in 1912 and disclosed in 1932, and #18 adopted in 1922 and disclosed in 1928. Seven of the companies dropped the policy and then reinstituted it. Of these, #9, #15, #17, and #19 switched their classification to the liability side of the Balance Sheet and resumed disclosing the amount of the contra asset account when it resumed that classification. Companies #4, #8, and #14 dropped the disclosure of the amount and then resumed it.

39 Amount of Depreciation Expense
Reported on the Income Statement

The separate disclosure of the depreciation expense amount in the income statement ranged from 1900 until 1937, with 10 of the companies dropping it and then 6 of these companies resuming the disclosure practice (see Table 14, Col. B, p. 83). Item 25 discussed the first mention of depreciation on the income statement, even though the amount of depreciation may not have been disclosed.

40 Change from Reserve for Depreciation
to Accumulated Depreciation

The terminology change from "reserve to depreciation" to "accumulated depreciation" took from 1934 to 1969 to happen (see Table 14, Col. C, p. 83).   By decades the breakdown was 1930's (1), 1940's (5), 1950's (7) and 1960's (7).   This was a substantial time later than the 1948 ARB #34 on the *Use of the Term "Reserve,"* which recommended that the term "reserve" not be used for the contra asset account.(12)

TOPIC V
INVENTORY

41 Year of Disclosure of Inventory Method

Eight of the 20 companies disclosed their inventory method in their first annual reports studied (see Table 15, p. 84). The lags between the first annual reports studied and the disclosure of the inventory methods followed by the other 12 companies were 16 years for #3, 33 years for #4, 31 years for #5, 3 years for #6, 2 years for #8, 6 years for #9, 1 year for #11, 27 years for #14, 47 years for #15, 2 years for #16, 10 years for #17, and 28 years for #19.

42 Inventory Methods

Various inventory methods have been compiled in Table 15. Four of the companies have used the sales price of their inventory for inventory valuation. It was stated in a note in the Auditors' Certificate for 1906 that the American Bank Note Company (#1) valued its inventory at selling prices. This policy was changed in 1908. Armour (#3) stated in its 1926 annual report that packinghouse products were valued at market values less allowances for selling expenses. Calumet & Hecla (#4) in 1934 valued "copper sold, not delivered" at selling price. Quincy Mining (#16) in 1863 recognized revenue when the copper was mined. This policy has continued through the years, although the effect of it is less important as the company has become more and more an investment holding company than a mining company.

39

Ten of the 20 companies utilized the cost basis for inventory at one time, while 18 used the cost or market, whichever was lower, method at various times. American Ship Building (#2) used cost plus anticipated profits from 1909 to 1915 for its work in progress inventory. Eight of the companies have used the fifo basis, while 9 companies have used the lifo basis. American Ship Building (#2) has adopted the percentage of completion method three times through the years.

Seven of the companies have utilized some other basis for inventory valuation. American Ship Building (#2) in 1900 stated that its amount for material inventory was valued at market value. Calumet & Hecla (#4) valued its copper at 9 cents per pound in 1884 but there was no indication given of the valuation basis. This policy of stating the cents per pound valuation of copper continued until 1917, as did the lack of indication of the valuation basis. General Electric (#8) adopted this basis in 1897:

> Raw materials have been valued at the market prices prevailing on January 31, 1897; active selling finished and partly finished apparatus and supplies at factory cost; inactive or slow selling apparatus and supplies at about 50 percent of factory cost; obsolete apparatus and supplies at scrap value; and tools, instruments, furniture, etc., at present value.

> The inventories of the factories showed an excess over book value of $141,184.98, which is not taken as a part of the year's profit, but is retained as a reserve.

In 1900, it took a further step toward conservatism by valuing raw materials "at the lowest price paid by the company during the last three months of the fiscal year."

International Harvester (#12) in 1918 adopted the base stock approach, but it was discontinued in 1921.

> The "basic" inventory representing a normal quantity of raw materials, work in process, and finished products has been valued at 1916 inventory prices (being the actual cost of that year), which were adopted in 1917 as a fair and stable basis for inventory valuations during the period of the war. The "excess" inventory (that is, the quality in excess of normal) has been valued at reasonable market prices. In addition, the company is carrying the general inventory reserve previously accumulated, which has been deducted from "net material purchases," etc., after close of manufacturing season.

. . .

The rapid decline in market values during the year 1921 of the commodities entering into the company's products has resulted in price levels that make unnecessary the continuation of the "basic" inventory method of valuing inventories; therefore, raw materials and supplies, including purchases after the close of the manufacturing season, have been valued at cost or market, whichever was lower, at December 31, 1921. Work in process of manufacture and finished products have been valued at replacement cost, based on market values of raw materials and labor rates at December 31, 1921, such replacement cost being lower than the year's cost of production.

Union Oil (#17) in 1913 stated that "The figures are of actual inventory. In arriving at them a basic price of 31 1/2¢ per barrel for crude oil was adopted, or 2 1/2¢ less than was figured in the balance sheet of December 31, 1912, although selling prices on crude oil average about 1 1/4¢ higher than in 1912. Present net prices at the well average from 36 1/2¢ to 45¢ for fuel oil." In 1914, it wrote, "All inventories of merchandise have been taken at figured cost or less." From 1935 to 1944, Union Oil utilized a base stock approach. It wrote in 1941 that

Since December 31, 1935, the principal commodities in the inventories have been priced at basic prices, plus approximate transportation and other costs; relatively unimportant revisions in such prices have been made from time to time to reflect changed operating conditions, but the basic prices presently used are substantially equivalent to those determined in accordance with costs prevailing at the end of 1935.

In 1945, it dropped the base stock approach and then in 1946 adopted the lifo method.

In 1893, U.S. Rubber (#18) labeled its inventory account as "value of rubber and other merchandise on hand, estimated." In 1903, the lower of cost or market procedure was adopted. United Fruit (#19) valued its sugar at market value in 1920 and in 1930 and 1931. In 1932, the lower of cost or market method was adopted.

43 Use of Inventory Reserves

Inventory reserves were very commonly used. Ten of the companies studied had utilized them. Diamond International in 1915 stated that "The management has deemed it advisable to create a reserve for $388,000 to be applied against the inventories of raw materials purchased at abnormal prices and thus provide, to some extent, against the decline in prices which will naturally follow the cessation of hostilities abroad." The amount of $192,000 was so reserved in 1917, and $300,000 was credited to a "reserve to protect stocks against price decline." In 1917, $1.7 million was added to this account. In 1947 and 1948, $1.5 million was appropriated from earnings for the "reserve for possible inventory price decline."

Kodak established in 1941 an inventory reserve of $2.5 million by a deduction from earnings so "to provide for a possible shrinkage in inventory values and for other unusual costs and expenses that may arise because of the war and the resultant regulations and restrictions." In 1942, $3.5 million was added to the reserve by an extraordinary charge to the income statement. In 1943, $4. million was so charged and $2.5 million in 1944. This reserve was almost totally reduced by charges in the years 1945 and 1946 for events due to wartime operations. General Electric, as discussed in item 42, established a reserve for $141,000 in 1897. Hart, Schaffner & Marx in 1941 deducted $100,000 from inventories to constitute a special reserve against possible changes in inventory values. This charge was a component of the profit of the parent company for the year. In 1913, International Harvester had a $900,000 depreciation provision from inventory. By 1915, this amount had risen to $1.25 million, and by 1918 to $5.975 million of war losses. International Harvester reclassified $15 million of its general reserve to an inventory reserve in 1932.

The deficit for the year made it necessary to transfer $10,000,000 from general reserves to surplus. These reserves, on which we also drew heavily in 1931, were established from earnings of prior years as a blanket protection against market declines in inventories throughout the world, decline in dollar exchange value of current assets in foreign countries, and other unforeseen contingencies. Years of experience have shown that a world wide business such as ours is subject to many contingencies and losses not predictable as to time, place, nature or extent. This policy of providing general blanket reserves has seemed to the management the best protection against such contingencies, and we are fortunate in having them available at this time; they are necessary insurance, operating for the benefit of both stockholders and customers and should be renewed when earnings again permit. The balance of these blanket reserves not yet used is $15,000,000. This has been applied in the balance sheet as a deduction from inventories, such inventories having been valued at cost or market, whichever was lower. How much of these reserves may be required to meet further declines in prices and foreign exchange rates depends, of course, on the economic conditions prevailing during the next few years.

In 1933, $10 million was written down to the inventory reserve; $3.5 million was added to the reserve in 1934. In 1936, $9 million was transferred from surplus to the inventory reserve and in 1937, $7.5 million was charged to the income statement for reserve. In 1941, $3 million was added to this reserve by a charge to the income statement and the reserve was reclassified as a liability reserve. In 1942, a special reserve for $5.5 million for regular inventories that are slow moving or subject to restrictions was deducted from inventory values. In 1943, $4 million was reduced from this reserve by a credit to cost of goods sold.

Kresge established an inventory reserve in 1941: "Experiences following the World War of 1914-1918 have caused action to be taken, through setting up a reserve of $1.083 million, to relieve or minimize the effects of post-war merchandise price adjustment which this experience shows are likely to occur. This action, although reducing the reported profits of the current year by 19¢ per common share, is believed to reflect with greater accuracy the long term results of operations during this abnormal period." In 1942, $1.341 million was added to the reserve, and in 1943, $0.756 million was added. In 1945, $0.252 million was debited to the reserve account "to offset the loss on certain merchandise considered to have become valueless or materially reduced in value with the end of the war." Nabisco in 1934 noted that there was a special inventory reserve for $1.017 million. In 1946, the inventory reserve was increased to $5 million because of high prices and unsettled conditions. The inventory reserve was reclassified from a contra asset account to a liability reserve. In 1956, this account was closed to unappropriated retained earnings. Union Oil in 1930 established a $2.5 million inventory reserve.

U.S. Rubber had numerous and somewhat unclear inventory reserve activities (see Table 16, p. 86).

In 1916, U.S. Steel established a charge to the income statement and a credit to inventory for $15.625 million for a "reserve for amount of actual cost or market value of stocks in excess of normal prices therefore." At 12/31/16, $13.525 million remained in the inventory account. This policy continued through the years. In 1929, the inventory reserve account was closed to surplus.

Year	Income Statement	12/31 Reserve
1917	$29.748 million	$30.271 million
1918	20.297 million	51.290 million
1919	38.710 million	90.000 million
1920	5.000 million	95.000 million
1921	not stated	60.710 million
1922	not stated	49.460 million
1923	1.078 million	51.220 million
1924	not stated	50.391 million
1925	not stated	50.143 million
1926	not stated	50.143 million
1927	not stated	48.016 million
1928	not stated	47.076 million

44 Write-downs of Inventory to Surplus,
to Income Statements, and to General Reserves

Table 17 (see p.87) deals with inventory write-downs to surplus, excluding U.S. Rubber activity described in Table 16. Seven companies, excluding those happenings already discussed in Item 43, used income statement and/or inventory reserve write-downs of inventory. Armour had a $9.5 million deduction for inventory price decline for non-lifo inventory items for 1946 and $8.0 million in 1947 for the same purpose. Calumet & Hecla in 1919 deducted an item "reduce to market value" for $249,000 in the income statement, $3.636 million in 1920, $687,000 in 1921, and $68,000 in 1922. DuPont wrote down its inventory valuation in 1920 by $10.342 million because of a drastic price fall. The write-down was charged to reserves for contingencies:

> A corresponding gain, which accrued to your interests during the prolonged period when prices were increasing, was not shown as a separate item, because of the difficulty of measuring it properly. However, your directors felt in the years 1917 and 1918 that a considerable decline in the value of inventories would in due course occur and, therefore, arbitrarily set aside out of the then current profits an amount estimated to be sufficient to meet such adjustments in inventory values and for other contingencies. Consequently, it is appropriate to write off the reduction in inventory against the fund so created without disturbing the profits for the year 1920.

In 1921, the amount of the write-down was $9.071 million, of which only $0.389 million was charged to earnings. General Electric wrote-down the book value of copper inventory by $2 million in 1908, because of a sudden and severe shrinkage in the value of copper. In 1920, $17.804 million write-down of inventories to market was made on the income statement. General Motors in 1920 and 1921 deducted on the income statement $18.502 million and $16.6 million, respectively, for "special write-offs and write-downs of inventory in excess of reserves available set up in previous years." In 1930, Union Oil reduced inventories by a $1.402 million charge to income. In 1931, U.S. Steel made inventory price adjustments of $5.396 million to a previously established contingency reserve. In 1932, $3.135 million was so charged, as was $7.468 million in 1933. In 1932, $13.935 million was charged to an extraordinary expense for unabsorbed overhead, rather than being charged to inventory. In 1933, $435,000 was charged against previously established reserves and $426,000 against a newly created reserve for inventory obsolescence. In 1933, $7.468 million, in 1934, $7.806 million, and in 1935, $7.719 million were the extraordinary charges for overhead.

45 Classification of Inventory

Two of the companies, Diamond International and United Fruit, had interesting histories of inventory classification. Diamond International in 1899 classified pine stumpage with more current assets but in 1907 no longer classified it as an inventory asset. In 1924, it returned to the inventory classification. This change was explained in the 1923 annual report:

> Notwithstanding the splendid showing presented by the general balance sheet in regard to working capital, liquid assets and current assets over liabilities, current and total, it may be well to call attention to the fact that the figures and division of the general balance sheet fail to show the real liquid asset resources of your company. In both the property account and foreign and domestic investments are assets that could be quickly converted into cash. The book value of timber as of December 31, 1923, stands at $3,505,826.09, and the timber, with its necessary and associated operating plants, is carried at $4,619,046.11. All of timber owned by your company is readily salable and could be disposed of within a few months' time at figures far in excess of stated book values.

In 1947, the account was reclassified as a deferred charge to operations.

United Fruit classified "Merchandise, stock on hand as per Inventories" as a component of fixed assets in the 1901 balance sheet. In 1914, sugar stock on hand was classified as a current asset. In 1924, the current asset caption for inventory became fruit and sugar stock on hand. In 1926, there were three types of inventories classified as current assets: sugar and other products, merchandise, and material and supplies. In 1939, materials and supplies were removed from current assets and returned to that classification in 1969. U.S. Steel in 1939 reclassified inventory of sundry operating parts, supplies, etc., from current assets to other assets.

TOPIC VI
VALUATION OF FIXED ASSETS

46 First Disclosure of Intangibles in the Balance Sheet

Table 18 deals with the year that the presence of intangibles was disclosed (see Table 18, p. 88). Of the 13 companies which disclosed that they had intangibles as a component of fixed assets, only 5 of these disclosed that fact in their first reports studied (see Table 18). The lag between the first report studied and the first disclosure ranged from 1 to 45 years. Two of these companies noted the amount of intangibles and then wrote them off in the same year. One can conclude that there was some reluctance to report intangibles separately from tangible fixed assets.

47 Write-ups of Fixed Assets

Table 19 deals with the write-ups of fixed assets (see Table 19, p. 89). Union Oil, #17, was the only company to have a systematic write-up practice for fixed assets. In 1922, it added $38.838 million to properties for "appreciation between cost and valuation agreed to with Natural Resources Division Internal Revenue Department of Oil Producing Properties at March 1, 1913" less $11.192 million for "appreciation formerly set up in the accounts." There appears to have been an addition to the contra asset account "reserve for depletion," so that the net amount credited to surplus was only $8.47

million.   In 1923, $20.428 million was added to a separate surplus account for "appreciation of new discovery areas brought in as providing territory, subsequent to March 1, 1913--less depletion accrued to December 31, 1923--the values of such properties for the purposes of depletion having been agreed upon with the Natural Resources Division of the Internal Revenue Department." In 1925, it was $15.334 million.   In 1926, $53.351 million was added to the properties account for "appreciation in value of proven oil properties." The surplus "arising from appreciation in value of proven oil properties" went to $47.218 million in the balance sheet as of 12/31/1926.   Price, Waterhouse stated in the Auditors' Certificate that "producing oil and gas territory is stated in the balance sheet at valuations determined by the company based upon the estimated recoverable oil and gas content."   The balance of this account on 12/31/1927 was $40.879 million, because of $6.339 million of depletion on appreciation for oil produced from lands previously appreciated in the accounts. No new appreciation was added in 1927. No change occurred in 1928 or in 1929. In 1930, the ending balance was $34.154 million. In 1931, it did not change but at the end of 1932, it was $32.831 million. In 1933, $1.207 million was decreased from this account.   In 1934, the appreciation account disappeared with this comment: "The appreciation of proven oil properties amounting to $31,624,365.86, which was shown under the caption of surplus at December 31, 1933, has been deducted from oil lands and development. This adjustment conforms with the current trend of accounting procedure and in no way affects the value of the company's oil properties."

There appeared to be some appraisal write-ups for these companies. Not one company credited income. In fact, two of the companies did not even credit a surplus account. The one company which had a write-up policy abandoned it after these major write-ups. The writer finds that the evidence offered here is not overwhelming either to prove or disprove the claims made that there were wholesale write-ups in the period from 1900 to 1929. Further work must be done to validate Carman Blough's statement that

The idea that "plant and equipment should be restated in terms of current replacement costs" whenever some significant event occurs, otherwise at "periodic intervals, perhaps every five years," is an old and discarded idea with only a slightly new twist. Shades of the 1920's! Those of us who remember how impossible it was to determine the fairness or reasonableness of the results of an appraisal shudder at the idea of going through it all over again. . . .(13)

48 Write-offs and Write-downs of
Book Values of Fixed Assets

This item is divided into the three segments of write-offs and write-downs to (1) surplus accounts (Table 20) (see p. 90), (2) earnings by extraordinary items (Table 21) (see p. 93), and (3) capital surplus accounts (Table 22) (see p. 94). The figures in Table 20 include adjustments for depreciation and amortization, as well as direct entries to the fixed asset accounts. Pullman (#15) wrote down a 1927 appraisal which was done for the reorganization of the parent and subsidiaries. Hence, this appraisal was not mentioned in Item 47. Union Oil (#17) and United Fruit (#19) both, at times, included amounts of miscellaneous debits and credits to surplus along with the adjustment to fixed assets. The writer assumed that the entire amount of the entry pertained to fixed assets. U.S. Steel's (#20) write-downs of intangibles of $30.205 million and $88.296 million pertained to the valuation of its founding in 1902 and, hence, this appraisal was not mentioned in Item 47.

The figures in Table 21 include adjustments for depreciation and amortization, as well as direct entries to the fixed asset accounts.

One point is evident from these tables: write-offs and write-downs of book value of fixed assets were not uncommon occurrences. The statement in APB #30 that write-down or write-off of intangible assets and losses on abandonment of property, plants, or equipment used in the business should not be extraordinary items can be better understood in this historical perspective.(14)

Another point is that most of the companies which recognized intangibles have written them off. This indicates some reluctance by management to retain these assets. American Ship Building (#2) recognized $6.684 million as goodwill and patents in 1914 and wrote the account off by a 1915 charge to surplus for $1.192 million, a 1930 charge to surplus for $3.492 million, and a $2 million charge to capital surplus in 1932. Armour (#3) amortized its $1.396 million goodwill account as a nonspecified income statement expense from 1935 through 1942. Diamond International (#5) recognized $5.917 million of patents, rights, and trademarks in 1907 and wrote that amount off by 7 charges to surplus from 1907 through 1917. General Electric (#8) wrote off its $8 million patents, franchises, goodwill account by 1908 through charges to surplus. Hart, Schaffner & Marx (#10) wrote off $5 million of its $15 million goodwill, trade names and trademarks account to surplus in 1920 and the other $10 million by a charge to capital surplus in 1935. IBM (#11) wrote down its patents and goodwill account to $1 by a $2 million charge to surplus in 1939 and a series of income statement ordinary charges from 1949 until 1957, when a charge of $4.918 million was made for such amortization on the income statement. Kresge (#13) in 1924 apparently wrote off the goodwill portion of its intangibles account. U.S. Rubber (#18) wrote its intangibles off by a charge to capital surplus in 1938, which was the same year U.S. Steel (#20) did write off its intangibles. Only two companies, DuPont (#6) and General Motors (#9), kept their intangibles accounts on the balance sheet as of December 31, 1969.

49 References to Appraisals

With the increasing reemphasis on the worth of current cost valuation techniques in financial accounting, the writer has included more detail on this matter than some of the other items. Most of the companies did not write up their fixed assets because of the appraisals but some did.

American Bank Note (#1) stated in 1934 that management apparently made an appraisal valuation in 1912.

> As of December 31, 1912 the aggregate value at which all properties were carried on the books of the company was segregated as between real estate, buildings, machinery, equipment, dies and rolls. Since that date all additions to real estate, buildings, machinery and equipment have been recorded at actual cost. In the case of dies and rolls the original value placed thereon in 1912 is considered by the management to represent a conservative valuation of these assets. All new dies and rolls made since December 31, 1912 have been charged to manufacturing costs in lieu of amortization of the original valuation assigned to this equipment at that date.

American Ship Building (#2) in 1914 wrote up real estate, dry docks, building, etc., by $1.137 million based on an appraisal by the Manufacturers Appraisal Company. Ernst and Ernst said in its first report as the public auditors of American Ship Building in 1916 that

> We have recommended to the officials of the company that a careful detailed appraisal be made of all of the fixed property of the company to establish present values and to assist the officials in determining proper amounts of depreciation.

> No change in the valuation of goodwill account has been made during the year and we have recommended to the officials that the valuation shown on the books be considered in connection with the appraisal of the physical assets hereinbefore commented on.

Armour (#3) reflected the ups and downs of the appraisal technique. There was a notation in the 1921 report that "the balance sheet shows an increase of approximately $23 million in fixed assets, $20 million of which is attributable to an appraisal of a portion of our buildings and machinery acquired when costs were extremely low. The appraisal made by outside appraisal companies brings these values in line with levels prevailing November 1, 1917, and which are substantially lower than present day replacement costs. The increase in value resulting from this appraisal was credited to surplus with the approval of Price, Waterhouse & Company, public accounts." This appraisal was done by the American Appraisal Company. An additional $9.625 million was added to surplus in 1922. By 1933, dividends on preferred stock were not made because of a fear that

> While the consolidated net income for the year exceeded the current dividend requirements on the preferred stocks of Armour and Company of Delaware and Armour and Company (Illinois), no dividend was paid on the preferred stock of the Illinois Company for the year as that the corporation law of Illinois prohibits an Illinois corporation from paying dividends unless its net assets are in excess of its stated capital, both before and after the dividend payment. Due to the general drastic decline in fixed property values during recent years, it is questionable whether the present value of the net assets of Armour and Company (Illinois) exceeds the stated capital. Counsel and auditors of the company have advised the directors that they therefore believe it not advisable to pay any dividends while this condition exists.

In 1934, $54.242 million was written off to surplus as a part of a capital reorganization for "reduction in book value of properties in respect to write-off of appreciated excess cost, loss of utility values, etc." In 1934, Calumet & Hecla (#4) disclosed that the valuation basis for mine lands was the depletable value allowed by the U.S. Treasury Department and for plants was the depreciable value allowed by the U.S. Treasury Department.

> Diamond International (#5) revised its valuation of fixed assets in 1907 based on an appraisal by the Audit Company of New York:

> The values of lands, buildings, machinery and equipment as appraised by this company December 31, 1906, have been placed on the books; to which had been added the actual cost of net additions during the year. From the value of the pine land and stumpage, as appraised by this company, has been deducted the sum of $703,496.97, owing to your Board of Directors not deeming it wise to enhance this value over cost; and from patents, rights, trademarks, etc., has been taken the sum of $917,370.61, both of which amounts have been written off against surplus.

Diamond International in 1924 disclosed a balance sheet based on an appraisal. It stressed, however:

> The value of the outstanding capital stock and surplus on this balance sheet, in which is incorporated certain revaluations based on 1924 appraisals, is $214.60 per share. The essential factors influencing and ultimately determining the value of capital stock are, however, not appraised values of plants and fixed assets, but (1) net earnings, and (2) excess current or liquid assets over all liabilities, hence the wisdom of writing down plant values, etc., to very conservative figures when gross earnings permit, reducing thereby the need of large depreciation deductions from gross earnings during periods of strenuous competition.

> The understating of property values--particularly plant values--in your company's published balance sheet and the conservative valuation of all assets on your company's books indicate sound business procedure. Every asset shown on the balance sheet is believed to be conservatively valued and there are no items whatsoever in inventory that are not readily salable and in excellent physical and marketable condition; your company's so-called quick or liquid assets are liquid in every sense of the word and, when disposed of, would show in the aggregate no loss due to shrinkage of values.

In 1929, an appraisal was done which showed a sound depreciated value of plant, machinery and equipment of $14.592 million and reproduction value of $18.980 million. In 1949, the company again commented on the undervaluation of the timberland account.

> Reference to the timber reserves owned by the company at December 31, 1949 is made on pages 3 and 1 of this report. The value at which these resources were carried at the end of 1949 averaged less than $2.00 per thousand board feet, a figure which is well below current market values and is conservatively related even to pre-war market values. It must be remembered that about 70 percent of this timber is located in California and was in large part purchased nearly 50 years ago. It is carried on the books of the company at cost less depletion which is a fraction of its current market value.

> DuPont (#6) in 1923 revalued its plant investment "on the basis of a uniform price level" by $5.805 million and credited that amount to the reserve for depreciation. In 1933, DuPont reported that an

appraisal study indicated that "in the values at which the fixed assets are now carried are substantially the same as current replacement cost." Hence, there was no adjustment made. In 1939, it wrote down properties held for sale by $1.161 million because their book values "were greater than present day values as indicated by appraisal." In 1893, General Electric used a valuation approach to justify the $8 million cost amount of its subsidiaries' patents, other valuable rights, licenses and other contracts.

> The transactions of your company are to a considerable degree with local companies working under contracts licensing them to use the patents, about 2,000 in number, under which your company operates. Your company is now supplying apparatus to about 1,300 local companies, the royalties from which run from $1,500,000 to $2,000,-000 per year. It is believed that the royalties will be greatly increased in the future, so that $8,000,000 would appear to be far within the actual value of the patents, contracts, etc., which are represented thereby.

Eastman Kodak (#7) in 1952 noted that "properties were valued at cost, which except for recent additions was much less than the current cost of replacement." In 1919, General Motors (#9) had the Manufacturers' Appraisal Company appraise fixed assets. General Motors then wrote up fixed assets by $29.889 million, which was balanced by a $22.929 million credit to goodwill, patents, copyrights, etc., and a $6.96 million credit to accumulated depreciation. International Harvester (#12) in 1907 went to great lengths to explain and defend its original valuation.

> The $120,000,000 capital stock as originally issued consisted entirely of common stock and was all fully paid for when issued; $60,000,000 was paid for in cash at par, and the remaining $60,000,000 was issued for the real estate, plants, and physical inventories acquired at organization which were conservatively valued by independent appraisers in excess of that amount, excluding any allowance for goodwill or patents. The real estate and plant properties were appraised by the American Appraisal Company and the Manufacturers' Appraisal Company. The raw materials, work in process of manufacture, and finished products were inventories under the supervision of and valued by Jones, Caesar and Company Certified Public Accountants. The ore mines, coal lands, and timberlands were surveyed and valued by competent engineers.

> No capital stock was issued or cash paid for the patents, trademarks, shop-rights, etc., which this company

received through the purchase of plants and properties at the time of organization. Those patents, trademarks, etc., were purchased, originated or established at great cost by the former owners during long and successful terms of business, and are a valuable asset of the company.

In 1924, Kresge (#13) wrote up "properties of subsidiary company in excess of premium paid on purchase of capital stock thereof" for $0.641 million. Pullman (#15) stated that on April 30, 1927, the "assets of the subsidiary companies were adjusted by appraisal to the basis of the plan of reorganization upon which these companies were taken over by Pullman Incorporated." The write-downs from 1932 through 1939 totaled $62.776 million. In 1943, $0.332 million was written off and as late as 1954, $4.487 million was written off for 1927 appraisal values. Quincy Mining (#16) discussed in 1957 its valuation of mining properties:

> Mine, mill and smelter property, plant and equipment are carried in the accounts at substantially the net amounts (basis as explained below less depreciation and depletion reserves) at which they were carried by the predecessor company prior to the reorganization in 1932 plus the cost of subsequent rehabilitation and betterment expenditures. The basis for these assets in the accounts of the predecessor company is believed to have been cost to that company, except in the case of mining property which was at March 1, 1913 valuation plus the cost of subsequent acquisitions and expenditures for mine development.

Union Oil (#17) in its 1903 list of resources noted the following valuations of "waterfront property in San Francisco, valued at $0.500 million," "agricultural or surface rights, 65,000 acres, not under the bonds, estimated value $0.400 million," and "120,000 acres of oil lands, which, by wells drilled at widely separated points thereon, have been proved to be immensely valuable, but at a mere nominal valuation of $50 per acre, amount to $6.000 million." Its auditors, Price, Waterhouse and Company, stated in its 1915 Auditors' Certificate that "The oil lands, rights and leases are stated at values considerably lower than those shown by independent appraisals in the company's files." In 1919, it was footnoted in the balance sheet that the valuation oil land, rights and leases did not include $79.313 million of appreciation of producing properties as of March 1, 1913. The appreciation amount was noted as being $78.781 million in 1920 and $57.351 million in 1921. As noted in Item 48, there were write-ups in 1922 and in 1926 and an eventual write-off by the end of 1934.

It was stated in the Auditors' Certificate in 1922 for U.S. Rubber (#18) that "the buildings and machinery owned by the company had a total appraisal value at December 31, 1922, after deducting depreciation accrued to that date, which was materially in excess of the value at which they are carried on the books." United Fruit (#19) contrasted in 1902 its book value of properties of $14.531 million to the appraisal value of $14.721 million. In 1904, it was stated that there was an excess of $560,000 of appraisal valuation of properties over book value. In 1910, this excess was $2.273 million. In 1930, the company noted it had placed on the books the appraised value of fixed assets of a new subsidiary. In 1932, Peat, Marwick and Mitchell aided United Fruit's staff in revaluing book values to conservative present day values. U.S. Steel (#20) in 1937 stated that the original valuation of its fixed assets "was based in part on the valuation assigned to these assets by the U.S. Bureau of Corporations in its survey and report on the formation of the corporation in 1901."

50 Goodwill Recorded as the Result of Acquisitions

Table 23 deals with the ending balance sheet amount of goodwill and the amortization policy of the companies listed (see p. 95). It shows wide differences in accounting practices in these companies.

51 Explanations of the Valuation of Intangibles

Two companies offered defenses for their intangibles policies. Diamond International wrote in 1917 that

> During 1917, our management decided to practically eliminate this account carrying it in the future at the nominal figure of $1.00, and this, not because our company's patents, rights, trademarks, secret processes, goodwill, etc., were not considered of value--for they are undoubtedly a valuable asset of our company--but because such a policy of listing assets was not considered good conservative accounting. Since January 1, 1918, the patents, rights, trademarks, etc., account has been steadily maintained on the books at the figure of $1.00, and all monies that have been paid out in research, machinery and process development work, the acquiring of patents, processes and improved production methods, etc., have been directly charged to operating expenses.

In 1929 it wrote that

> Management's policy has consistently been to refrain from capitalizing the sums expended from time to time in the development of, or acquisition of rights to use, mechanisms, processes, methods, formulas, etc., or in the

acquiring of patents and securing of either manufacturing
or sales rights. Aside from the value of patents, rights,
etc., it is well to bear in mind that the name and goodwill
of our company is a valuable asset, augmented as it is by
48 years of business success and by an undisputed
reputation today for equitable dealings and the production
of only reliable, safe and absolutely guaranteed quality
products--never more than rightly and fairly priced,
considering the cost of production and distribution, and
always within range of any competitive offerings.

General Motors defended its policy in 1921:

> The item of "goodwill, patents, copyrights, etc." has
> increased only $2,046,922 since 1919 to a present total of
> $22,370,811. From this it must not be concluded that this
> account is considered of small or doubtful value; in fact,
> these intangible values might be rated, conservatively,
> equal to the manufacturing plants; for the two items it
> would be much easier to replace the latter than to build
> up the goodwill and organization now enjoyed and con-
> trolled by General Motors Corporation. The coordination
> of departments and facilities, the development of ac-
> counting practice and prompt reporting on all subjects,
> the systematizing of manufacture and sales, the selection
> of a sufficient and capable personnel, the loyalty and
> effectiveness of sales and manufacturing organizations,
> all developed during recent years, have added greatly to
> the goodwill value of the tangible assets; in fact, the
> latter would quickly return to lifeless materials were it
> not for the livening influence of the intangible values
> classed as goodwill. However, these intangibles remain
> without material increase in their expressed values on the
> balance sheet, after several years of painstaking develop-
> ment.

52 Immediate Write-offs of the Valuation of
Tangible Fixed Assets

Eight of the companies adopted the policy of immediate write-
offs of tangible fixed assets. American Bank Note wrote off $33,000
of new machinery in 1906. In 1934, it stated that since 1912, it has
expensed "all new dies and rolls made since December 31, 1912 . . . in
lieu of amortization of the original valuation assigned to this
equipment at that date." In 1954, the company noted that dies and
rolls are to have "cost of additions charged to income currently."
Diamond International wrote in 1909 that renewals and replacements
were charged to operating expenses and that only additions and

improvements and construction of new plants and equipment were capitalized. Quincy Mining started in 1864 a policy, which ended in 1937, of charging some of the expenditures on "additions to permanent investment" to the profit and loss statement. As an example of this policy, the company stated in 1893 that "from the past year's earnings, $150,000 have been paid on account of purchase of 640 acres of land adjoining over mine, and containing at greater depth, the mineral deposit we are now working, known as the Pervalic view."

Pullman wrote off the "amount expended in rebuilding and remodeling old style cars in latest standard Pullman cars, and for discount on old cars sold" on the income statement from 1875 to 1883. In 1884, it started to debit surplus for this item. The total surplus deduction from 1884 through 1896 for this item was $0.728 million. Union Oil prior to 1951 expensed its exploration expenditures. It was noted in the 1902 Auditors' Certificate of U.S. Rubber that "in lieu of depreciation for the year all betterments and improvements to the plants of the companies have been charged to expense." From 1902 through 1911, United Fruit charged betterments to current operating accounts. U.S. Steel from 1902 to 1929 wrote off $207.709 million of capital expenditures to earnings and surplus, "thus substituting tangible property values in lieu of this amount of investment cost based on par of U.S. Steel securities originally issued as stated."

TOPIC VII
OTHER MATTERS

53 Introduction of Public Auditors

Six of the 20 companies immediately adopted the policy of employing public auditors (see Table 24, p. 96). The remaining companies had a time lag between the first year studied and the employment of a public auditor: #2 (9 years), #3 (12 years), #4 (31 years), #5 (6 years), #6 (3 years), #8 (5 years), #9 (7 years), #10 (3 years), #14 (35 years), #15 (47 years), #16 (77 years), #17 (9 years), #18 (5 years), and #19 (19 years). It is obvious that public auditors were not quickly accepted by a majority of these 20 companies.

54 Auditor Changes

Ten of the 20 companies kept their same auditors for the period studied (see Table 24, p. 96). Three of the companies have only changed auditors once, while 3 changed auditors twice. Three companies changed auditors 4 times over the years. Only one company adopted a rotating policy for its auditor and even this company, DuPont (#6), had only two auditors in the last 24 years studied. It is obvious that the concept of auditor rotation has not been a practice commonly followed.

59

55 Sample Auditors' Certificates

The writer chose 9 of the companies' Auditors' Certificates for this sample. The auditors of American Bank Note Company apparently had no difficulty certifying different bases of inventory valuation in 1906 and 1908. In 1906, the auditors stated that unfinished work was appraised at selling value and in 1908, "At the close of the year the inventories of work in progress, which had formerly been carried at selling value, have been, with our entire approval, written down to cost."

Ernst & Ernst felt no compulsion about recommending in 1916 that American Ship Building conduct an appraisal of all fixed assets "to establish present values and to assist the officials in determining proper method of depreciation" and that the valuation of goodwill should be examined. The auditors of Armour permitted a 1922 balance sheet to be issued which included the past balance sheet event of "the issue and sale of $50 million bonds and $60 million preferred stock of Armour and Company of Delaware since consummated, and the application of the proceeds in payments of gold notes and debentures of Armour and Company of Illinois (which have been called for redemption) and the reduction of other indebtedness as contemplated by the plan of financing."

The Audit Company of New York stated in its 1907 Auditors' Certificate that it had conducted an appraisal of Diamond International fixed assets as of December 31, 1906:

> The values of lands, buildings, machinery and equipment as appraised by the company, December 31, 1906, have been placed on the books to which has been added the actual cost of net additions during the year. From the value of the pine land and stumpage, as appraised by this company, has been deducted the sum of $703,496.97, owing to your Board of Directors not deeming it wise to enhance this value over cost; and from patents, rights, trade marks, etc., has been taken the sum of $917,270.61, both of which amounts have been written off against surplus.

Arthur Andersen stated in its 1943 Auditors' Certificate for DuPont that "The company maintains a combined surplus account which includes earned surplus, paid in surplus, and surplus arising from revaluation of assets. In our opinion the respective amounts of these different classes of surplus should be stated separately." Since DuPont had been rotating auditors and kept Arthur Andersen for 2 more years, it is probable that DuPont did not take a retaliatory step against its auditors. In 1947, Lybrand, Ross Brothers & Montgomery stated that DuPont had not followed generally accepted accounting principles when it deducted a $20.9 million provision for excessive construction cost. Lybrand continued as auditors for DuPont until 1954.

General Electric's auditors, Patterson & Corwin, gave a very detailed description of its audit program in its 1898 Auditors' Certificate. Some examples were:

> The technical nature of the business of the company, and the wide range, number and variety of the articles manufactured, render it impracticable for any persons not mechanically expert in the various lines and familiar with the goods, to correctly identify and inventory them; therefore, the inventories at January 31, 1898 were necessarily taken and priced by the company's own experts. We, however, noted the manner in which the inventories were compiled, item by item, and verified the computations. Our knowledge of the instructions given and the methods and precautions followed to insure correctness leads us to believe that said inventories were carefully and conservatively taken and that the amount carried over in the balance sheet fairly represents the value of the goods.
>
> We have not attempted to appraise the manufacturing plants, but in our opinion, which is based upon our observation of the methods of treating improvements to the plants and the amounts charged off for depreciation for extensions, the policy of the management regarding charges to plant is conservative.

> As to the value of the patents and franchises, we are not competent to express an opinion.

> We observed the instructions given and the precautions taken to enter all existing current liabilities on the books at the time of closing and are satisfied that all known accounts payable of the company are included in the balance sheet.

International Harvester's auditors, Haskins & Sells, commented in 1914 that "Adequate reserves have been provided for depreciation of fixed assets and for losses, except extraordinary losses or expenses which may result from the European War." In 1918, the auditors made this comment about International Harvester's base stock approach:

> We find that raw materials and supplies, work in process of manufacture and finished products were valued, generally, at 1916 prices (adopted in 1917 as a fair and

stable basis for inventory valuation during the period of
the war) for the portion of the inventories equivalent in
quantity to the 1917 inventories, and for the remainder, at
values considered by the company as reasonable market
prices. The general inventory reserves previously accumulated have been applied in reduction of such inventories.

Union Oil's auditors, Price Waterhouse and Company, approved
in 1915 of showing the values of "oil lands, rights and leases at values
considerably lower than those shown by independent appraisals in the
company's files." In 1922, it said that "producing oil and gas territory
at March 1, 1912, is stated in the balance sheet at the valuation
agreed upon with the Natural Resources Division, Internal Revenue
Department." In 1926, the wording was "producing oil and gas
territory is stated in the balance sheet at valuations determined by
the company based on the estimated recoverable oil and gas content."
However, in 1945, Price Waterhouse made the strongest comments
noted in this study.

During 1945 certain items have been charged and
credited directly to earned surplus account. In our
opinion, it would have been preferable if the following of
such items had been passed through the statement of
operations for 1945 as special charges and credits: The
charge of $5,188,373 for accelerated amortization appli-
cable to that year; credit of $1,157,600 being the portion
of the credit from reversal of the reserve for wartime
contingencies allocable to 1945 on the basis of accelerated amortization applicable to the respective years;
credit of $1,444,962 from gain on sale of properties by the
Canadian subsidiary; and credit on $1,500,000 representing
the reduction of the reserve for income taxes. If this
treatment has been followed, the charge against 1945
operations for Federal and other taxes on income would
have been reduced from $1,600,000 to $300,000 and the
latter amount shown as a special charge, the profit for
1945 before special charged and credits would have
appeared as $10,801,123 and the balance of profit trans-
ferred to earned surplus account would have appeared as
$9,415,312.

Price, Waterhouse was not Union Oil's auditor in 1946. This was the
only instance in which a conflict with the auditors apparently caused
a dropping of that firm in the following year.

United Fruit's auditors in 1919 apparently did not examine
foreign subsidiaries, as the auditors wrote that the statements "have
been correctly prepared from the books of the United Fruit Company

and from reports and records of subsidiary companies on file in the office of the company's general auditor." U.S. Steel's first Auditors' Certificate in 1902 included the wording "in our opinion the balance sheet is properly drawn up so as to show the true financial position of the corporation and its subsidiary companies, and that the relative income account is a fair and correct statement of the net earnings for the fiscal year ending that date." In 1947, Price Waterhouse held that replacement cost depreciation was not a generally accepted accounting principle. In 1958, Price Waterhouse stated that U.S. Steel's treatment of pension costs was not comparable with that of the past and that the effect on net profit after taxes was a $46.6 million overstatement. Despite these controversies, Price Waterhouse remained the auditors of U.S. Steel.

56 Placement of Income Taxes on the Income Statement

Twelve of the companies had their last placement of income taxes as a distribution of profit, while the remaining 8 considered this item to be an expense (see Table 25, p. 97). Since only companies #11, #13, #16, and #19 have not changed their placement through the years, one can safely conclude that uncertainty has existed on this item in practice and some rethinking about this item is probably warranted.

57 Deferred Income Taxes

All 20 companies used the deferral of income taxes approach and 5 of these companies apparently adopted this method in 1968 as required by APB #11 (see Table 25, p. 97).

58 Notes to the Accounts

Two companies have always included adequate explanations to the accounts. The range between the first year in the study and the first year of adequate explanations shows the apparent reluctance of managements to come to grip with this fact of disclosure (see Table 26, p. 98). The lags were: #1 (56 years), #2 (42 years), #3 (39 years), #4 (50 years), #5 (10 years), #6 (21 years), #7 (32 years), #8 (2 years), #9 (31 years), #10 (52 years), #11 (53 years), #13 (29 years), #14 (48 years), #15 (71 years), #16 (77 years), #17 (10 years), #18 (39 years), and #19 (2 years).

59 Disclosure of Earnings Per Share

Earnings per share disclosure ranged from 1923 to 1959 and apparently was a common practice in annual reports (see Table 26, p. 98).

60 Investment Credit

Twelve of the companies followed in 1969 the approach of reducing income tax expense for the investment credit. Five followed the deferral approach, while 3 companies had no disclosure of the procedure (see Table 26, p. 98).

61 Funds Statement

Table 27, funds statement, deals with the years that informal or formal funds statements were issued by the 20 companies (see p. 99). The writer used the criteria of proximity to the balance sheet and the income statement as the chief basis for deciding the formality of the presentation. A formal presentation was one in which the funds statement appeared to be included with the balance sheet and the income statement as major statements. Three of the companies did not issue a funds statement during the period of the study. Twelve of the companies disclosed formal type of funds statement in 1969. One company dropped its portrayal of the funds statement in 1960. What is surprising was the U.S. Steel (#20) issued a funds statement in 1902. The remaining companies took a long time to do this.

62 Treasury Stock

Table 28 shows that 19 of the companies had treasury stock at one time or other (see p.100). Only 3 of these companies classified it on the balance sheet consistently through the years, while the remaining 16 companies switched from either the asset or the contra-equity position. Clearly the trend was away from the asset placement, even though 3 of the companies had such a placement in 1969.

63 Use of the Term "Retained Earnings"

Nine of the companies switched to the term "retained earnings" from 1945 through 1949; 5 switched in the 1950's; the remaining 6 companies had switched by 1966. The years were #1 (1960), #2 (1959), #3 (1947), #4 (1960), #5 (1951), #6 (1966), #7 (1947), #8 (1949), #9 (1950), #10 (1953), #11 (1957), #12 (1946), #13 (1948), #14 (1949), #15 (1966), #16 (1963), #17 (1946), #18 (1962), #19 (1949), and #20 (1945). This showed again how long it took the companies to adopt a recommendation in ARB #39 in 1949 that "The term earned surplus be replaced by terms which will indicate source, such as retained income, retained earnings, accumulated earnings, or earnings retained for use in the business...."(15)

Conclusion

In conclusion, the writer suggests that these implications for financial accounting should be noted from this study. Management abuse of earned surplus/retained earnings was not proven by this study, whereas there was at least an indication of abuse of extraordinary items on the income statement. FASB might relax, rather than tighten, its restrictions on the use of retained earnings, while keeping its rigidity on the issue of extraordinary items on the income statement. The same uncertainty about how to handle the inflation/depreciation issue existed in the late 1940's as exists today. Confusion on this topic may be endemic to the inflation/depreciation issue. While the issue of whether significant write-ups of fixed assets occurred in the 1920's is unproven, the one instance of a consistent application of write-ups of fixed assets, Union Oil, should be analyzed to ascertain what happened and what were the effects on users.

Auditor changes are rare, and auditor rotation, obviously, will not occur unless mandated by the SEC. It is also quite clear that a significant number of managers feel that dividends on preferred stock, and some would go as far as dividends on common stock, are to be treated as expenses. Accountants need to do much more studying of this issue. Prepaid expenses may not be treated as a current asset because management may consider prepaid expenses to be more clearly an other asset. Accountants may be out of step on this issue. Lastly, much rethinking has to occur about foreign subsidiaries in the late 1970's. The differences in accounting for foreign subsidiaries noted in this study may again be endemic to the problem and not subject to a uniform solution. Those who are of the opinion that "reserve accounts" have been used to smooth income are supported by this study. Accountants should examine how disclosures of past appraisals were made, in the light of the great increase of interest of replacement cost.

The writer considers the implications for financial accounting significant enough to recommend that an institutional project be undertaken to expand this study from its 20 companies to 40 or 50 companies, so that a larger base be established for possible decision-making purposes. There are at least 20 or 30 more companies with reports at the Baker Library that could be analyzed along the lines of this study.

NOTES

[1]American Institute of Accountants,*Accounting Survey of 525 Corporate Reports (Fiscal Years Ending July 1946 to June 1947)* (New York: AIA 1948).

[2]Louis Goldberg, *An Inquiry into the Nature of Accounting,* American Accounting Association Monograph No. 7 (Iowa City: American Accounting Association), pp. 79-80.

[3]Eldon S. Hendriksen, *Accounting Theory,* 3d ed. (Homewood, Illinois: Richard D. Irwin, Inc., 1977), p. 294.

[4]Earl A. Saliers, ed.,*Accountants' Handbook* (New York: Ronald Press Company, 1947), p. 330, Illustrating the Federal Reserve Board Form of Balance Sheet.

[5]Committee on Accounting Procedure, American Institute of Accountants,*Current Assets and Current Liabilities: Working Capital,* Accounting Research Bulletin #30 (New York: AIA, 1947), p. 247.

[6]Committee on Accounting Procedure, AIA,*Comparative Statements,*ARB #6 (New York: AIA, 1940), p. 49.

[7]Ibid.,p. 50.

[8]Committee on Accounting Procedure, AIA,*Accounting for the Use of Special War Reserves,*ARB #26 (New York: AIA, 1946), p. 217.

[9]Committee on Accounting Procedure, AIA,*Accounting Treatment of General Purpose Contingency Reserves,*ARB #28 (New York: AIA, 1947), pp. 231-32.

[10]Committee on Accounting Procedure, AIA, *Income and Surplus,*ARB #32 (New York: AIA, 1947), pp. 260-61.

[11]Accounting Principles Board, *Reporting the Results of Operations,*Accounting Principles Board Decision No. 9 (New York: American Institute of CPAs, 1966), p. 111.

[12]Committee on Terminology, AIA,*Use of the Term "Reserve,"* ARB #34 (New York: AIA, 1948), p. 273.

[13]Carmen G. Blough, "Comments," in Robert T. Sprouse and Maurice Moonitz' monograph.*A Tentative Set of Broad Accounting Principles for Business Enterprise,*Accounting Research Study #3 (New York: American Institute of CPAs, 1962), p. 62.

[14]Accounting Principles Board,*Reporting the Results of Oper-ations—Reporting the Effects of Disposal of a Segment of a Business, and Extraordinary, Unusual and Infrequently Occurring Events and Transactions,*Accounting Principles Board Decision No. 30 (New York: American Institute of CPAs, 1973), p. 566.

[15]Committees on Accounting Procedure and Accounting Ter-minology, *Accounting Research and Terminology Bulletins,* final ed. (New York: American Institute of CPAs, 1961), p. 136, Appendix A, and p. 31, Accounting Terminology Bulletins.

TABLES

Table 1
Balance Sheet Data

Co #	1st Yr.	Format				Comp. BS	P/E OA	P/E CA	1st Ment. CA
		FA 1st	CA 1st	CA-CL	Other				
1	1906	1906	1935			1954–1969	1906		1906
2	1900	1900	1916			1960–1969	1916	1959	1914
3	1910	1918 1910	1927 1922	1947		1931–1933 1947–1969	1922		1910
4	1884		1923 1950	1947	1884 1900	1950–1969	1934	1923 1960	1915
5	1899	1899	1924 1961	1948		1910–1969	1920	1913	1913
6	1907		1907			1907–1914 1916–1920 1948–1969	1920	1950	1922
7	1902	1902	1929	1947		1933–1969	1904	1947	1902
8	1893	1893 1907	1901 1933			1928–1969	1933	1917	1917
9	1911	1911	1920			1913–1969	1935	1911	1911
10	1911	1911	1924			1945–1969	1911 1934	1924 1948	1911

11	1911		1911			1955-1969	1912	1961	1912
12	1907	1907	1928	1946		1939-1969	1907		1907
13	1912	1913	1959 / 1912 / 1934			1943-1969	1913	1926 / 1960	1913
14	1899	1899 / 1875 / 1906	1927 / 1925	1953		1946-1969	1934 / 1934 / 1939	1925	1927 / 1925
15	1875				1900	1939-1969			
16	1861	1861	1937 / 1911 / 1934 / 1966	1945	1861	1966-1969	1937	1948	1937
17	1903	1903 / 1912	1893 / 1917		1903	1942-1969	1912	1957	1912
18	1893	1902				1896-1901 / 1936-1941 / 1944-1969	1917		1917
19	1900	1900	1926			1901-1925 / 1956-1969	1900	1959	1900
20	1902	1902	1939	1945		1936-1969	1939		1902

Table 2
Valuation Bases of Marketable Securities

Co #	Cost	Cost or Less	MV	LcM	Par	Est RV	Lower Par/ MV	MV or Less
1	1934		1906					
2	1909	1910	1918		1926			
3						1922		
5		1933						
7	1943	1915	1931					
	1953	1941	1950					
	1957		1955					
8				1944			1931	
12	1943			1933				1931
				1955				
13	1934	1931						
14			1933		1935			
17	1937		1931					1932

Table 3
Income Statement Data

Co #	1st Year	Years IS	Comp. IS	Rev. on IS
1	1906	1906-1969	1954-69	1954-69
2	1900	1916-1969	1960-69	1960-69
3	1910	1910-1919	1931-33	1937-69
		1923-1969	1947-69	
4	1884	1917-1969	1950-69	1917-69
5	1889	1907-1969	1910-29	1938-69
			1949-69	
6	1907	1907-1969	1907-13	1907-35
			1916-20	1937-69
			1924	
			1926-69	
7	1902	1930-1969	1933-69	1935-69
8	1893	1893-1969	1926-69	1894-69
9	1911	1911-1969	1913-69	1933-69
10	1911	1911-1969	1945-69	1911-12
				1945-69
11	1911	1912-1969	1955-69	1936-69
12	1907	1907-1969	1907-08	1907-12
			1938-69	1935-69
13	1912	1912-1912	1912-12	1912-12
		1926-1969	1940-69	1926-69
14	1899	1926-1969	1948-69	1945-69
15	1875	1875-1969	1929-69	1875-69
16	1861	1861-1969	1966-69	1861-1969
17	1903	1909-1910	1915-22	1934-69
		1912-1969	1942-69	
18	1893	1896-1918	1936-41	1902-18
		1931-1969	1944-69	1931-69
19	1900	1900-1969	1901-25	1956-69
			1956-69	
20	1902	1902-1969	1903-69	1902-69

Table 4

Use of Earned Surplus and Use of Extraordinary Items

Co #	First Year	Earned Surplus				Income Statement			
		# of Debits	# of Credits	In thous Debit Amounts	in thous Credit Amounts	# of Debits	# of Credits	in thous Debit Amounts	in thous Credit Amounts
1	1906	9	6	$ 1,921	$ 1,409	57	10	$ 6,742	$ 2,580
2	1900	43	29	28,930	23,232	37	6	10,471	1,841
3	1910	40	20	163,594	44,913	18	8	53,020	13,413
4	1884	7	9	2,066	1,051	1	0	358	0
5	1899	29	25	20,634	22,930	30	4	10,716	11,205
6	1907	10	31	481,779	544,859	13	13	51,208	22,268
7	1902	15	7	34,846	30,817	8	2	15,750	11,540
8	1893	30	23	57,492	201,754	13	7	143,916	87,000
9	1911	8	1	12,530	200	3	6	42,075	219,023
10	1911	8	10	8,118	3,909	10	1	1,715	230
11	1911	38	8	45,867	64,485	14	0	2,422	0
12	1907	8	25	86,562	140,305	10	10	52,168	25,217
13	1912	15	23	12,117	10,616	5	3	4,262	1,575
14	1899	1	8	4,714	19,462	9	3	6,534	7,874
15	1875	124	20	97,873	52,783	5	3	6,929	13,075
16	1861	14	9	893	116	9	1	806	4
17	1903	51	14	44,157	76,097	6	3	4,123	4,329
18	1893	49	9	104,021	16,077	65	8	124,546	8,932
19	1900	58	26	198,806	85,942	5	0	21,376	0
20	1902	34	25	307,629	201,878	4	5	36,928	12,964
		591	328	$1,714,549	$1,542,835	322	93	$596,065	$443,070

Table 5
Schedule of Companies with Greater Dollar Amounts of
Debits to Credits in Earned Surplus

Co #	in thous $ Debits	in thous $ Credits	Ratio of $ Debits to $ Credits
1	1,921	1,409	1.36 to 1
2	28,930	23,232	1.25 to 1
3	163,594	44,913	3.64 to 1
4	2,066	1,051	1.97 to 1
7	34,846	30,817	1.13 to 1
9	12,530	200	62.25 to 1
10	8,118	3,909	2.08 to 1
13	12,117	10,616	1.14 to 1
15	97,873	52,783	1.85 to 1
16	893	116	7.70 to 1
18	104,021	16,077	6.47 to 1
19	198,806	85,942	2.31 to 1
20	307,629	201,878	1.52 to 1

Table 6
Schedule of Companies with More Debits
than Credits for Possible Income
Statement Items in the Earned
Surplus Account

Co #	Number of Debits	Number of Credits	Ratio of Number of Credits to Number of Debits
1	9	6	1.50 to 1
2	43	29	1.48 to 1
3	40	20	2.00 to 1
5	29	25	1.16 to 1
7	15	7	2.14 to 1
8	30	23	1.30 to 1
9	8	1	8.00 to 1
11	38	8	4.75 to 1
15	124	20	6.20 to 1
16	14	9	1.56 to 1
17	51	14	3.64 to 1
18	49	9	5.44 to 1
19	58	26	2.23 to 1
20	34	25	1.36 to 1

Table 7
Schedule of Companies with at Least
2-to-1 Ratios in Either One of the
Tests of Surplus Items

Co #	$ Ratio	# Ratio	Both
3	3.64 to 1	2.00 to 1	Yes
7	1.13 to 1	2.14 to 1	No
9	62.65 to 1	8.00 to 1	Yes
10	2.08 to 1	0.80 to 1	No
11	0.71 to 1	4.75 to 1	No
15	1.85 to 1	6.20 to 1	No
16	7.70 to 1	1.56 to 1	No
17	0.58 to 1	3.64 to 1	No
18	6.47 to 1	5.44 to 1	Yes
19	2.31 to 1	2.23 to 1	Yes

Table 8
Comparison of $ of Debits to $ of Credits
for Companies with Greater $ Debits than $ Credits
for Extraordinary Items on Income Statement

Co #	in thous $ of Debits	in thous $ of Credits	Ratio of $ Debits to $ Credits
1	$ 6,742	$ 2,580	2.61 to 1
2	10,471	1,841	5.69 to 1
3	53,020	13,413	3.95 to 1
4	358	0	infinite
6	51,208	22,268	2.30 to 1
7	15,750	11,540	1.36 to 1
8	143,916	87,000	1.65 to 1
10	1,715	230	7.46 to 1
11	2,422	0	infinite
12	52,168	25,217	2.07 to 1
13	4,262	1,575	2.71 to 1
16	806	4	201.50 to 1
18	124,546	8,932	13.94 to 1
19	21,376	0	infinite
20	36,928	12,964	2.85 to 1

Table 9
Comparison of # of Debits to # of Credits
for Companies with the same or More Debit than Credit
Entries for Extraordinary Items on Income Statement

Co #	# of Debits	# of Credits	Ratio of Debits to Credits
1	57	10	5.70 to 1
2	37	6	6.17 to 1
3	18	8	2.25 to 1
4	1	0	infinite
5	30	4	7.50 to 1
7	8	2	4.00 to 1
8	13	7	1.86 to 1
10	10	1	10.00 to 1
11	14	0	infinite
13	5	3	1.67 to 1
14	9	3	3.00 to 1
15	5	3	1.67 to 1
16	9	1	9.00 to 1
17	6	3	2.00 to 1
18	65	8	8.13 to 1
19	5	0	infinite

Table 10

Schedule of Companies with at Least
2-to-1 Ratios in Either One of the Two
Tests for Extraordinary Items of Income Statement

Co #	$ Ratio	# Ratio	Both
1	2.61 to 1	5.70 to 1	yes
2	5.96 to 1	6.17 to 1	yes
3	3.95 to 1	2.25 to 1	yes
4	infinite	infinite	infinite
5	0.96 to 1	7.50 to 1	no
6	2.30 to 1	1.00 to 1	no
7	1.36 to 1	4.00 to 1	no
10	7.46 to 1	10.00 to 1	yes
11	infinite	infinite	infinite
12	2.07 to 1	1.00 to 1	no
13	2.71 to 1	1.67 to 1	no
16	201.50 to 1	9.00 to 1	yes
17	0.95 to 1	2.00 to 1	no
18	13.94 to 1	8.13 to 1	yes
19	infinite	infinite	infinite
20	2.85 to 1	0.80 to 1	no

Table 11
Depreciation Matters

Co #	First Year Study	Depr First Ment	Year Meth Noted	Method (P) Partial	Placement Contra Asset	Placement Liab Side
1	1906	1906	1934	Tax	1927	
2	1900	1901	1969	SL	1927	
3	1910	1912	1967	SL	1933	
			1934	Tax		
4	1884	1917	1958	SL to Use (P)		
			1960	Other (P)	1923	
5	1899	1900	1918	SL or Use	1915	1909
			1959	SL to SYD (P)		
			1965	Back to SL		
6	1907	1909	1948	SL to ACC	1965	1915
7	1902	1902	1954	SL to SYD (53)	1914	1904
8	1893	1894	1967	ACC (61)	1894	
9	1911	1911	1954	SL to ACC (53)	1914	1913
					1940	1920
10	1911	1912	1963	Tax	1913	
			1968	ACC		
			1969	ACC and SL		
11	1911	1911	1956	SL to SYD (56)	1912	
			1943	Tax		

12	1907	1907	1964	SL to SYD (P)	1913	1907
			1966	ACC/Tax		
			1969	ACC to SL		
13	1912	1912	1935	Tax	1912	
14	1899	1899	1954	SL to ACC (53)	1899	
			1954	Tax		
			1966	ACC to SL (66)		
15	1875	1900	1937	ICC/SL	1914	1906
			1941	SL to Use	1927	1926
			1968	ACC (54)		
			1969	SL (54)		
16	1861	1917	1917	Tax	1937	
			1948	Use (P)		
17	1903	1904	1930	SL to Use (P)	1916	1911
			1943	SL		
			1954	SL to ACC (P)	1931	1926
			1963	ACC to SL (63)		
18	1893	1896	1934	Trade	1922	1912
			1953	SL		
19	1900	1900	1926	Use	1932	1947
					1954	
20	1902	1902	1908	Use	1910	1902
			1948	SL to ACC		
			1957	Tax		
			1968	ACC to SL		

Table 12
Description of Amounts for Depreciation

Co #	Term	Text	Auditors
1	"adequate"	1934	
5	"ample"		1907-38
6	"sufficient"	1909	1910
7	"ample"		1902-24
8	"liberal"	1911	
10	"adequate"	1931	
11	"adequate"	1913	1915
12	"adequate"		1907-33
14	"adequate"	1938	
15	"sufficient"		1922
17	"ample"	1913	
	"adequate"		1915
18	"not fully provided"		1922
19	"liberal"	1900	
	"careful"	1902	
20	"sufficient"		1908

Table 13
Emergency Write-off Provisions

Co #	Year Mentioned	Year Written Off
6	1944	1945
	1952	
7	1945	1945
	1951	
8	1941	1945
	1951	
9	1940	
	1951	
16	1943	
17	1945	1945
	1953	
18	1945	1945
	1953	
20	1942	1945
	1952	

Table 14

Amount of Accumulated Depreciation (or Reserve for Depreciation)
Shown on Balance Sheet as a Contra Asset (Col. A), Amount of
Depreciation Expense Reported on the Income Statement (Col. B),
Reserve for Depreciation to Accumulated Depreciation (Col. C)

Co #	A Years	B Years	C Years
1	1927-69	1906, 1912-54	1954
2	1931-69	1916-69	1960
3	1933-69	1923-69	1954
4	1923-45, 1961-67	1917-53, 1966-67	1947
5	1915-69	1921, 1932-37, 1948-69	1952
6	1965-69	1931-69	1965
7	1930-69	1930-66	1969
8	1917-53, 1956-69	1906-09, 1932-69	1949
9	1918-19, 1940-69	1920-69	1948
10	1913-69	1912-13, 1917, 1945-69	1950
11	1912-69	1912-15, 1922-69	1966
12	1913-69	1907-10, 1916-44	1964
13	1932-69	1926-69	1948
14	1899-1918, 1944-69	1926-67	1934
15	1914-25, 1929-69	1900-1918, 1921-28, 1930-69	1950
16	1937-69	1937-61	1961
17	1916-25, 1931-69	1912-18, 1934-69	1949
18	1928-69	1926-45, 1961-69	1962
19	1932-46, 1954-69	1932-69	1954
20	1910-69	1902-69	1954

Table 15
Inventory Matters

Co #	First Year Study	First Year Ment	Methods								
			Sales Price	Cost	LCM	Cost Plus	Fifo	Lifo	Aver Cost	% of Comp	Other
1	1906	1906	1906	1908, 1916, 1946, 1961	1934, 1917, 1931	1909	1966				1900
2	1900	1900							1957	1942, 1957, 1967	
3	1910	1926	1926		1926		1942, 1959A	1941P, 1947P, 1950P, 1951P			
4	1884	1917	1934P	1917	1962		1952P				1884
5	1899	1930			1930						
6	1907	1910			1910						
7	1902	1902		1902	1915		1949	1945P, 1951P			1897
8	1893	1895		1895	1949			1955A			1900
9	1911	1917			1917		1947				
10	1911	1911			1911						
11	1911	1912		1912	1916		1941		1952		
12	1907	1907			1907, 1921						1918

Firm	(1)	(2)	(3)	(4)	(5)	(6)	(7)	(8)	(9)
13	1912	1912			1912	1964	1950P		
14	1899	1926			1926				
15	1875	1922		1922	1951	1951P	1951P		
16	1861	1863	1863						
17	1903	1913		1927	1914 1928		1945		1913 1930 1935
18		1893			1903			1941	1893
	1893								
19	1900	1928		1928	1932		1941		1920
20	1902	1902		1902			1947		1930

P: A use of that method for a part of the inventory.
A: Indicates that a firm previously using more than one method switched to one method.

Table 16
U.S. Rubber's Use of Inventory Reserves
and Inventory Write-downs

Year	Amount		Account
1912	$ 0.500	million	Reserve for contingencies decrease
1914	1.500	million	Write-down
1917	1.000	million	General inventory reserve increase
1918	?		Inventory adjustment
1920	11.154	million	Write-off to general inventory reserve
	6.000	million	Increase inventory reserve
1921	10.000	million	Decrease inventory reserve
	2.023	million	Decrease inventory reserve
	4.091	million	Surplus write-down
	6.425	million	Reserve write-down
	6.594	million	Surplus write-down
	6.000	million	Reserve write-down
1924	1.500	million	Write-down
1925	2.007	million	Surplus write-down
1926	3.000	million	Reserve write-down
	8.535	million	Reserve increase
1927	8.535	million	Reserve write-off
	8.911	million	Surplus write-off
1928	15.038	million	Write-down on income statement
1930	11.084	million	Write-down to surplus
1931	1.574	million	Write-down to surplus
1937	3.000	million	Write-down to inventory reserve
	0.648	million	Write-down to income statement
1938	1.175	million	Write-down to income statement
1951	1.239	million	Write-down to income statement

Table 17
Inventory Write-downs to Surplus,
Other than U.S. Rubber

Co #	Year	Amount in thous
2	1921	$ 588
	1924	266
3	1941	(147)
	1944	227
8	1894	2,158
9	1911	2,000
	1912	2,834
	1913	4,728
10	1918	300
	1931	473
	1931	358
11	1914	77
	1920	160
12	1936	(3,938)
	1936	766
17	1912	241
	1923	2,010
	1930	2,500
	1931	4.919
	1931	2,291
19	1930	7,000
20	1915	500
	1910	500
	1917	4,000
	1933	1,000
	1941	(415)

Table 18

First Disclosure of Intangibles in the Balance Sheet

Co #	First Year Study	First Year Disc	Account Title	(in millions) Amount
2	1900	1914	Goodwill, patents, as per books	$ 6.684
3	1910	1935	Goodwill less amortization	1.396
5	1899	1907	Patents, rights, trademarks	5.917
6	1907	1920	Patents and goodwill	?
6	1907	1931	Patents, goodwill, etc.	24.884
7	1902	1902	Goodwill and patents	?
7	1902	1914		write-off
8	1893	1893	Patents	8.000
9	1911	1911	Goodwill	7.664
10	1911	1911	Goodwill, trade names, and trademarks	15.000
11	1911	1912	Patents and goodwill	?
11	1911	1926	Patents and goodwill	13.649
13	1912	1912	Goodwill, leases, etc.	4.376
14	1899	1944	Intangibles	write-off
18	1893	1928	Intangibles	58.205
20	1902	1937	Intangibles	260.369

Table 19
Write-ups of Fixed Assets

(in millions)

Co #	Year	Amount	Account Debited	Account Credited
2	1914	$ 1.137	Plant & property	Appreciation of Real Estate, dry docks, buildings, etc.
3	1921	20.000	Buildings and machinery	Surplus
	1922	9.625	Buildings and machinery	Surplus
5	1907	?	Buildings and machinery	?
		?	Patents, rights, trademarks	?
		?	Pinelands and stumpage	?
6	1923	5.805	Plants	Reserve for Depreciation
9	1919	29.889	Fixed assets	Reserve for depreciation
13	1924	0.641	Fixed assets	Goodwill
17	Various--See separate explanation.			Surplus

Table 20

Write-offs and Write-downs of Book Values
of Fixed Assets to Surplus

Co #	Year	Description	Tangible (in millions)	Intangible (in millions)
1	misc	4 debits	$ .832	$
2	misc	15 debits, 5 credits	7.943	
	1915	Goodwill		1.192
	1930	Goodwill		3.492
3	misc	3 debits	8.530	
	1934	Write-off of appreciated excess cost	54.242	
	1959	Replacement and relocation of facilities	43.788	
5	misc	4 debits	2.204	
	misc	7 debits		5.917
6	1931	Patents		5.354
7	1941	To offset entire book value of goodwill and patents		15.798
	1931	Excess of cost over tangible assets at acquisition		3.717
	misc	Excess of cost over tangible assets at acquisition 2 debits		.345

No.	Date	Description		
8	misc	5 debits	1.638	
	1899	Reduction of book value of patents, franchise and goodwill		4.000
	misc	Reduction of book value of patents, franchise and goodwill, 6 debits		6.577
9	misc	2 debits tangible, 1 debit intangible	1.596	.972
10	misc	1 debit tangible, 1 debit intangible	1.555	5.000
11	misc	1 debit tangible, 8 debits intangible	.241	2.654
13	1924	Goodwill, written off adjustments of book value, 1 debit, 3 credits	(2.340)	4.062
14	1944	Intangibles		4.714
15	misc	83 debits, 2 credits	19.346	
	1932	Adjustment of asset values	23.445	
	1939	Write-off of balance of 1927 appraisal, increase in valuation of carrier properties	33.143	
16	misc	3 debits, patents and goodwill	.272	
17	misc	5 debits, 1 credit	15.388	2.358
18	misc	9 debits	34.037	
	misc	12 debits		

19	misc	18 debits, 1 credit	29.907	
	1931	Future write-downs of property	10.000	
	1932	Reserve for revaluation of fixed assets	50.945	
	1960	Expropriation of Cuban assets	22.281	
	1960	Write-down of tropical banana facilities	27.103	
20	misc	7 debits, 8 credits	16.924	
	1928	Amortization of appreciated cost in excess of their investment in tangible property		30.205
	1929	Amortization of appreciated cost in excess of their investment in tangible property		88.296
			$403.020	$184.653

Table 21

Write-offs and Write-downs of Book Values of
Fixed Assets to Earnings by Extraordinary Items

Co #	Year	Description	Tangible (in millions)	Intangible (in millions)
1	misc	3 debits	$ .200	$
2	misc	20 debits	5.816	
3	1966	Replacement or relocation of facilities	2.400	
5	misc	11 debits	1.865	
6	1947	Investment in excess of acquired equity in subsidiary		.907
7	misc	Provision for excessive construction cost	20.900	
10	misc	4 debits	3.250	
11	misc	2 debits, 1 credit	(.153)	
12	1937	12 debits	.864	
14	misc	Provision for abandonment of ore mine	.850	
15	1923	Write-down of plants, real estate, machinery, intangibles, etc.., 7 debits	4.353	?
16	misc	Addition to reserve for depreciation	.671	
18	misc	2 debits	.070	
		6 debits	15.093	
			$56.179	$.907

Table 22

Write-offs and Write-downs of Book Values of
Fixed Assets to Capital Surplus

Co #	Year	Description	(in millions) Tangible	(in millions) Intangible
2	1932	Goodwill		$ 2.000
3	1933	Land	$ .074	
10	1935	Goodwill		10.000
14	1944	Intangibles		9.656
15	1954	Net write-down of the car rying values of land to Cost	4.487	
18	1938	Goodwill, patents, etc.		57.662
20	1938	Intangibles		260.369
			$4.561	$336.687

Table 23

Goodwill Balance as the Result of Acquisitions

Co #	Year	(in million) Goodwill Amount	Amortization Policy
3	1965	($12.600)	Amortized 7 1/2 years
4	1957	0.403	Unamortized until 1960, then 10 years
5	1959	0.907	Unamortized, written off in 1962
	1960	4.061	Unamortized
	1962	3.160	
7	1967	14.029	Amortized over 15 years
9	1911	7.664	Unamortized
	1918	35.715	Unamortized
	1919	20.234	Unamortized, part written off
	1969	63.442	Unamortized
11	1964	17.019	Amortized from 1964 through 1967
14	1965	26.506	Unamortized
15	1945	1.076	Unamortized until write-off in 1947
17	1950	1.038	Unamortized until 1951, then over 5 years
18	1961	1.657	?
	1965	6.344	?
19	1966	14.532	Amortized over 5 years
	1965	4.255	Unamortized
	1966	6.936	Unamortized
	1968	19.589	Unamortized
	1969	41.522	Unamortized

Table 24
Public Auditors

Co #	First Year of Study	First Year of Audit	Auditor Changes	Years of Tenure
1	1906	1906	0	64
2	1900	1909	2	7, 52, 2
3	1910	1922	0	48
4	1884	1915	4	5,2,21,18,9
5	1899	1905	4	1,25,21,10,8
6	1907	1910	21	1,2,1,1,1,1,1,2,1,1,1,1,1,1,1, 1,1,2,9,4,3,8,16
7	1902	1902	0	68
8	1893	1898	2	8,4,60
9	1911	1918	0	52
10	1911	1914	0	56
11	1911	1911	4	4,1,6,11,37
12	1907	1907	0	63
13	1912	1912	0	58
14	1899	1934	0	36
15	1875	1922	0	48
16	1861	1938	1	21,11
17	1903	1912	1	34,24
18	1893	1898	1	4,68
19	1900	1919	2	1,12,38
20	1902	1902	0	68

Table 25
Treatment of Federal Income Taxes

Co #	Expense	Distribution of Profit	Deferral
1	1917-33	1934-69	1962
2	1918-24	1917	1963
		1925-69	
3	1917-36	1937-43	1958
	1944-69		
4	1923-35	1917-22	1960
		1936-67	
5	1948-60	1917-47	1962
		1961-69	
6	1941-69	1926-40	1968
7	1933-34	1930-32	1965
		1935-69	
8	1917	1918-20	1963
	1921-40	1941-64	
	1965-69		
9	1941-69	1917-40	1968
10	1918-36	1917	1968
	1938-42	1937	
	1945-51	1943-44	
		1952-69	
11		1918-69	1964
12	1935-37	1938-62	1957
	1963-69		
13		1917-69	1958
14	1931-47	1926-30	1962
	1951-69	1948-50	
15	1918-26	1927-40	1963
	1941-47	1948-69	
16		1956-69	1965
17	1923-42	1917-22	1968
	1945-69	1943-44	
18	1913-16	1917-69	1956
19		1917-69	1960
20	1909-35	1936-42	1968
	1943-69		

Table 26
Miscellaneous Matters

Co # Co #	First Report in Study	Notes to Account First Year of Explanation	Earnings Per Share First Year of Notation	Investment Credit Asset Offset	Investment Credit Deferred Credit	Income Tax Expense Reduction
1	1906	1962	1947		1962-63	1964-69
2	1900	1942	1960			1965-69
3	1910	1949	1947		1962	1963-69
4	1884	1934	1952		1962	1963-67
5	1899	1909	1925		1962-63	1964-69
6	1907	1928	1926		1963-69	
7	1902	1934	1931		1962-63	1964-69
8	1893	1895	1926		1962-69	
9	1911	1942	1923		1962-69	
10	1911	1963	1959	Not noted		
11	1911	1964	1928		1962-69	
12	1907	1907	1944	1962	1963	1964-69
13	1912	1941	1937			1962-69
14	1899	1947	1948	1962	1963-69	1964-69
15	1875	1946	1929	Not noted	1962-63	
16	1861	1938	1938	Not noted		
17	1903	1913	1925	1962	1963	1964-69
18	1893	1932	1940		1962-63	1964-69
19	1900	1902	1929	Not noted		
20	1902	1902	1949		1964-67	1968-69

Table 27
Funds Statement

Co #	First Year in Study	Years Informal	Years Formal
1	1906		1964-69
2	1900		1966-69
3	1910	1949	1969
		1958-68	
4	1884	1964-67	
5	1899	1949-54	1948
		1956-61	1962-69
6	1907	Not noted	
7	1902	1943-44	1965-69
		1957-64	
8	1893	1954-69	
9	1911	1920	1967-69
		1963-66	
10	1911	1961-69	
11	1911	Not noted	
12	1907	1950-59	
13	1912		1964-69
14	1900	1949-66	1967-69
15	1875		1964-69
16	1861	Not noted	
17	1903	1915-35	1963
		1956-62	1965-69
		1964	
18	1893	1947-57	1967-69
		1961	
		1964-66	
19	1900	1961-69	
20	1902		1902-69

Table 28
Treasury Stock

Co E	Assets	Contra Equity
1	1930-43	1944-45
2	1931-42	1953-69
3	1931-42	1968-69
	1956-67	
4		1955-67
5	1899-1900	1925-47
6	1934-38	1925-38
	1947-56	1943-46
7	1932-34	1909-20
	1956-69	1927-52
		1959-63
8	1936-69	
9	1921-69	1911-19
10	1931-42	1911-19
		1943-69
11	1929-50	1915-16
12	1932	1931-52
	1964-68	1964-69
13	1929-33	1934-47
		1964-69
14	1934-39	1966-69
15	1931	1932-46
16		1952-69
17	Not noted	
18	1910-27	1909
	1940-41	1928-37
		1961-69
19	1927-61	1920-21
		1957-69
20	1929-42	1943-47
	1948-?	

UNIVERSITY OF FLORIDA ACCOUNTING SERIES

No. 1   Financial and Managerial Reporting by Certified Public
        Accountants
        62 pp., 1963
        *A collection of papers concerning the accountant's report
        to management, as well as financial projection through
        accounting.*

No. 2   Annotated Bibliography of Electronic Data Processing
        52 pp., 1968
        *The revised edition of a comprehensive bibliography which
        contains entries on over 60 books and 300 articles from
        professional journals up to December 31, 1967.*

No. 3. The American Accounting Association--Sponsored Statements
        of Standards for Corporate Reports, A Perspective by Harvey
        T. Deinzer
        52 pp., 1964
        *Comparative analyses of the four major Statements of
        Accounting Principles issued by the American Accounting
        Association, in 1936, 1941, 1948, and 1957.*

No. 4   Aspects of Contemporary Accounting
        83 pp., 1968
        *An examination of several topics related to problems encoun-
        tered in contemporary accounting, such as estate planning,
        macro-accounting, and absolutism.*

No. 5   Methodological Presuppositions in Financial Accounting Models
        by Harvey T. Deinzer
        99 pp., 1968
        *An organization of accounting doctrines and patterns in
        reference to assumptions about the conditions for knowledge.*

No. 6   Theory Formulations
        edited by Williard E. Stone
        97 pp., 1970
        *A survey of the historical development of accounting postu-
        lates and suggestions toward the development of accounting
        principles for specific purposes.*

No. 7   Foundations of Accounting Theory
        edited by Williard E. Stone
        163 pp., 1971
        *A series of papers presented by twelve distinguished
        accounting scholars investigating both the theoretical and
        applied natures of accounting and providing an understanding
        of the total systems aspect of accounting.*

No. 8   The Accountant in a Changing Business Environment,
        edited by Williard E. Stone
        82 pp., 1973
        *Papers presented for discussion in the University of Florida
        Distinguished Accountants Seminar Series, 1970-72.*